95

WH CARES WHAT I THINK?

American Teens Talk About Their Lives and Their Country

Edited by
Marcia A. Thompson

Close Up Publishing

D0428083

Library of Congress Cataloging-in-Publication Data

Who cares what I think? : American teens talk about their lives and
  their country / edited by Marcia A. Thompson.
      p.   cm.
    ISBN 0-932765-49-1 : $10.95
    1. Teenagers—United States—Interviews. 2. Teenagers—United
States—Social conditions. I. Thompson, Marcia A.
HQ796.W477   1994   93-35903
305.23'5'0973—dc20   CIP

Copyright 1994
Close Up Foundation
Printed in the United States of America
All rights reserved.
98 97 96 95   5 4 3 2

The Close Up Foundation, founded by Stephen A. Janger in 1971,
is a nonprofit, nonpartisan educational organization dedicated to
encouraging citizen involvement in government through
Washington-based seminar programs for high school and middle
school students, teachers, and older Americans.

For information about Close Up programs, call 800-256-7387. For
information about Close Up publications, call 800-765-3131.

"Atticus was right. One time he said you never really know a man until you stand in his shoes and walk around in them. Just standing on the Radley porch was enough."

—Scout, from *To Kill A Mockingbird*

Contents

Preface

$\mathcal{T}$he image of American teens today is somewhat of a caricature in many adults' eyes. Society tends to label them the "MTV generation," with a short attention span. We focus on what they're not learning and assume many don't know when the Civil War was. We compile statistics on their SAT scores, the numbers who drop out, the numbers who carry guns to school. But these generalizations tend to ignore individual teens who are struggling to make sense of the events around them. Having worked with teens in the classroom and in recreation programs, I knew their image was selling them short. The everyday teen that makes up the heart of our society is much more than that.

The best way to find out what they're really like was to go out and talk with real teens. The ones I contacted were thrilled to be interviewed, describing it as everything from "cool" to "the most important thing I've ever done in my life." A serious national forum for teens to talk about their lives and their country seemed long overdue.

The Close Up Foundation is a nonpartisan, nonprofit organization, so our goal in this project was to provide a forum. Close Up does not endorse any particular view and is not pushing any particular political agenda with this book. We were not looking for specific answers from the interviewees, and I made that clear to them at the time we talked.

Students were selected with the help of teachers and others who knew them. I sought teens from a broad range of backgrounds in American life today— some familiar, such as a middle-class teen with a job; some less familiar, such as a teenage migrant worker; and some notorious but little understood, such as a gang member. With only sixteen spaces to fill, this collection obviously is more of a snapshot than a scientific sampling.

I wanted students to be comfortable and to be themselves for the interviews, so I usually interviewed them and took their photographs in their home-towns. Thus, it seemed appropriate to cluster the chapters by the geographic environment in which I met the interviewees—the city, the country, or the suburbs. Though I worked from the same base of questions, I varied them slightly to relate to their individual lives. The words here are their own, but the interviews were edited and restructured for clarity.

I like and respect every person I interviewed. The experience had me laugh-ing, gasping, and sometimes crying. I was inspired many times by these kids' courage, forthrightness, and resilience. In other instances, I was alarmed by their experiences, factual errors, or radical ideas. The contrast shows a tremendous diversity in lifestyle, socioeconomic status, and overall outlook on life in the United States. The most fascinating aspect for me was trying to discover how each person's individual experiences contributed to his or her attitude and lifestyle. On a larger scale, the words of these young Americans celebrate the successes and highlight the problems in raising citizens who can positively contribute to our diverse and ever-changing society.

Most of these teens hold strong opinions about society and government, even though they sometimes lack information. Many think the government could be doing a better job in areas such as the economy, discrimination, urban problems, education, and homelessness. Not surprisingly, every teen expressed at least a little distrust of politicians (whether or not they could describe what politicians do). Gang member Damion says incredulously, "Would I trust them? No. If they was doing the right thing, there wouldn't be so much crime in Los Angeles."

One experience that several of the teens shared was that of discrimination. While most people commonly think of discrimination against women and discrimination against African Americans, these teens saw discrimination in many forms. Pharoah, an African American, talks about sitting down on the bus and watching people get up and move away from him. Keith expresses frustration that bright Asian Americans are being limited from entering top schools. Cynthia not only worries about hearing people discriminating against deaf people, but fears that deaf people are discriminatory toward hearing people. Kat comments on being discriminated against on the streets of Baltimore because she was a white girl, and therefore none of the African Americans wanted to buy drugs from her. Several teens also raise the issue of gay rights. Many urge their peers and others to forget about skin color and other differences, and treat each other as brother and sister. As Anitra says, "We're all people."

Despite their complaints, most are proud to be Americans and wouldn't live anywhere else in the world but the United States. As Dan says, "I love the United States, because as many negative things or as many picky things as I've said about the way our country works, in reality it's one of the most for-ward-thinking, democratic countries in the world."

One striking consistency is the effect of the presence or absence of strong adult role models in their lives. In talking about life in the projects, Pharoah says, "[K]ids need somebody to push them. It's really because of my mama pushing me . . . that's why I'm different from my friends." Without anyone to "push" them, several teens developed dangerous and even criminal lifestyles.

I hope that political leaders especially pay attention to what these teens have to say. These soon-to-be-adults are poised to become the next generation of workers, professionals, parents, and leaders. Some teens feel estranged from the political system. Some perceive the government as unrepresentative. Some can't identify how the government affects them. Before it's too late, we have to ask ourselves, have we invested enough? A U.N. declaration states, "Mankind owes to the child the best it has to give," because in the words of Marian Wright Edelman, "[D]oing what is right for children and doing what is necessary to save our national . . . skin have converged." In a democracy, not only do we want them to grow up healthy and strong, but also to believe that who they are and what they think matters.

Acknowledgments

One of the most exciting and rewarding aspects of developing this book was the enthusiastic support from almost every person who heard about it. There were many people instrumental in helping me identify interviewees: Alex Kotlowitz in Chicago, Illinois; Carmen and Al Legge in Mission, Texas; Marcel Lewinski in Northlake, Illinois; Jim Donlevy and Gary Payne from the Edwin Gould Academy in Chestnut Ridge, New York; Deputy Probation Officer Steve Wells from the Centinella Area Probation Office in South Central Los Angeles; Evangelina Peña and Maria Luisa Vasquez in Baytown, Texas; Lois Barnes in Frankfort, Kentucky; Heather Collins in Lower Brule, South Dakota; David Seiter and Jan Rawlins from Northridge High School in Layton, Utah; Tom Knapp and Bob Andrian from the Loomis Chaffee Academy in Windsor, Connecticut; Mary Lou Hobbs from the Fellowship of Lights in Baltimore, Maryland; Judith Chagrin and Laura Ash-Brackley from the Baltimore County Department of Social Services; Dr. Roger Tom in San Francisco; Marian Bowen of Vienna, Georgia; Kenneth Vidato and Ana Maria Soto of the Close Up Program for New Americans; Kathy Okerlund of Close Up's Educational Outreach Department; Karol Strang, Coordinator of County, Agency, and School Services in Brunswick, Maryland; and Kelli Hill and Hill's Gymnastics in Gaithersburg, Maryland.

Many members of the Close Up staff helped make this possible. Director of Publications Lynn Page Whittaker conceptualized this project and supported it in every possible way; Vice President of Programs Chuck Tampio supported us in a new venture for Close Up Publishing; Judy Myers designed the book and the cover with ever-versatile skill; Steve Waxman panicked whenever necessary to ensure production to a "T"; Kimberly Couranz and Anne Myers Kendrick copyedited and proofread the manuscript; Amanda Blythe Dramstad and Amy R. Rowland researched selected topics and copyedited early drafts; Vivian Watson and intern Jill Jankowsky helped with transcriptions; Cindy Graff Hobson gave interviewing tips; and Renée Bouchard offered crucial photography advice. Thanks to the rest of the Close Up Publishing staff for their patience. A fond thanks goes to the academic publications unit of Tiffany Larbalestier, Tim Walker, Linda Monk, and Chuck Sass for getting me on my feet, supporting the project, and being willing to help at all times.

Developing this book gave both Lynn and me a renewed appreciation for the importance of supportive role models in one's formative years. For listening to us and encouraging us when we were teens, Lynn thanks her parents, Josephine Smith Page and the late Herbert Page, and teachers June Powell, Linda Maddox, Betty Lytle, and Marian Bowen; and I thank my parents, Sandra Thompson and the late Berney Thompson, and teachers Rita Morgan, Paul Haskell, and Rusty Clauss.

Finally, the most important recognition of all goes to Pharoah, Cynthia, Kat, Keith, Damion, Elizabeth, Stan, Anitra, Sylvia, Holly, Gerardo, Rhett, Caine, Cindy, Dominique, and Dan and their supportive families. Their willingness to share their lives and thoughts with others is one of the best examples of generosity I've ever seen. I for one learned a great deal from them, and I can truly say that I am different person for the experience. Thanks.

About the Editor

A native of the state of Virginia, Marcia A. Thompson holds a bachelor's degree from the University of Virginia and a masters in education from George Mason University. She has worked with teenagers in the classroom and in youth programs, and has developed educational materials in high school social studies as a staff member of the Publications Department of the Close Up Foundation.

In the City

Help them help themselves.

Pharoah Walton

Fourteen-year-old Pharoah Walton enjoys watching the Chicago Bulls, reading the newspaper, rollerskating, talking on the phone, and going to game arcades with friends. Pharoah spent the first thirteen years of his life in the Henry Horner public housing project near the Bulls stadium and only one mile from the booming downtown of Chicago. Pharoah and his family were the subject of Alex Kotlowitz's 1991 bestseller, There Are No Children Here, a description of two years in the midst of drug wars, gang violence, fear, and poverty. Pharoah's intelligence, cheerfulness, and determination helped him to survive in the projects. Now, in part with the help of Kotlowitz's friendship, Pharoah has moved out of the projects and is attending Providence-St. Mel, a private school dedicated to the education of 500 African-American students. Pharoah thus straddles two very different worlds that exist side by side in America today.

***W**as all of the violence in the projects caused by gangs?* Well, not all of it, but maybe 95 percent of it was.

***W**hy do you think the gangs are so violent?* Fighting over territory—which is dumb. Life at Henry Horner was real bad. I've seen a lot of killings, shootings. Many of my friends have gotten killed, stabbed, stuff like that.

Sometimes life there was fun; sometimes we made it fun. Like going to the stadium to Bulls games. We got in by slipping in. It's really bad what we did [*looking sheepish*], but we'd get in line with a father and kids and we'd get right in front of the father. So the father would be looking after his kids, and the ticket lady would say to us, "Where's your ticket?" and we'd say [*pointing back to the father*], "He's got it." Then, all of us would run through. When she'd get to the father, he'd say, "I don't have it." But by that time we'd be upstairs where they couldn't find us.

One thing we'd do for money was watch cars outside the stadium while their owners were inside at the game. We were supposed to make sure nothing happened to the cars. But here's how it really worked. Kids—about eight of them—would run real fast when a car comes up because only the first one or two to the car would get paid. Sometimes the person in the car gets scared and drives off. But other times, the driver will roll down the window, and we'll say, "Can we watch your car, sir?" And he'll say, "Yeah." But we really don't watch the cars. By the time he gets in the stadium, we'll like be at home, looking at TV. Then about twenty minutes before the stadium lets out, we go back and make sure nothing has happened to the car and collect the money. Some of them will pay before the game and after—give you two dollars now and two dollars later. Some only after.

My only regret of going to the stadium was how scary it was in the dark. The game starts at 7:30 and ends at like 10:30, so we wouldn't get back until 11:00. When we'd leave, my mama would walk us out of the building, but then on the way back, all the lights would be off, all the lights in the whole building, so you can't see nothing. The lights were supposed to be on, but the robbers knock them out every day, because they like to rob people.

I'd spend the money I made on junk food. Or I'd try to save up my money, so like when a new pair of shoes came out, I could get them. I love to get new shoes! Once I'd saved up like eighty dollars. And one day, I don't know who it was, but someone must have found where I kept my money in my house, and they took it. And I never saved it up again, because that really hurt. I was so mad.

*D*id you have any other way of getting money? No, not really. The big-time drug dealers, they would offer me and some of my friends a lot of money—like forty dollars for two hours—for standing on security. Just to watch out for the police. And if the police come, you don't say, "The police are coming." You gotta say, "Five-O coming," or "Diana coming," so the police won't know we are referring to the police. I never did that, but some of my friends did. I stayed out of it because my mama told me about it, so I was prepared to resist.

If I were a parent with kids, I'd try to help them resist by trying to make it sound as bad as possible. I'd tell them while they were young. I'd also say, "I'll get you all you need," and stuff like that. In the projects, you can't get all you need. You can't afford it.

I haven't been back to the projects in like a year or so. I worry a lot less now because my family is out of the projects. They have a new nice house, and my mom's going to get her own business. I used to worry about them so much that it was interfering with my school. Now, I think about them sometimes, but it's nice that my whole family's doing better.

I still have friends who live in the projects. It's like in the movie *Boyz N The Hood*. That's what it kind of reminded me of. This one boy reminded me of the leader, the big guy, played by Ice Cube, because now he's selling drugs. And all the rest of them are in some kind of trouble. I think of myself as like, you know, that boy that got shot at the end, but he'd got his test scores back and got into college. I don't think of myself as being shot, but as going on to college.

*D*o you think your friends are going to make it? Un-uh. I don't think so.

*W*hat do you think would help people like your friends from the projects? What would you do? You need to start taking care of the problem when the problems first begin. Like, kids need somebody to push them. It's really because of my mama pushing me—like when I was younger, making me stay in the house and do my homework. That's why I'm different from my friends. But if I had stayed in the projects, I wouldn't have been as smart as I am now, because most of the kids in the projects don't even go to high school. That's real bad. Most of their moms are dope addicts, and stuff like that.

But you can't do everything for a person. First, you've got to help them help themselves. But I'd try to do whatever I can. I would like to help them. If I were a top businessman, I'd have a lot more pro- grams, like the Boys Club. The Boys Club used to be where kids who had a membership card, they'd go there, and have to spend an hour on their homework before any recreation. And now that's stopped. I don't know why. Now the Boys Club is just all fun; it's not doing any- thing for the kids to help them with school. I'd have other programs, like day camp, to try to get kids to like school.

One program I don't like is welfare. When you have one baby, then you get 100 dollars. Then when you have two, you get 150. So let's say the parent is on drugs; they're going to keep on having babies, so they can get more money. I don't think the system is set up right. It should be if you are a pregnant teen- ager, and you're going to school, then you get more money for one baby than a dropout gets who also has one baby. Or something like that.

The Henry Horner Homes is one of Chicago's nineteen public housing developments. In 1987, when Pharoah was nine, 6,000 people lived in Horner's sixteen high-rises. Of these residents, 4,000 were children. Officially, unemploy- ment was 19 percent; unofficially, much higher. An average of one person was beaten, shot at, or stabbed every three days.

I think people who are try- ing to help themselves should be able to get wel- fare, not as like income, but for a limited time until they find work, say for maybe eight months to a year. And if you haven't found work by then, obviously you haven't been looking too hard, or you don't want to work, or something like that. I just don't think welfare's set up right.

One thing that people your age and a little older have been criticized for is not really caring about what's going on and not being interested in current events and politics. Do you think that's true? That's sort of true. Most of my friends at school are not into politics and stuff like that. Usually, on every test we have an extra credit question. Like who is Ross Perot or someone else, and stuff like that. And usually just 20 percent of the class gets it. So that kind of shows that most kids—I won't say most, but a lot of kids nowadays—aren't too keen on current issues.

I'm not sure if they care what's going on with the community, in Chicago. Some of the kids in my school are from rich black families, from all over the city of Chicago. There aren't a lot of wealthy black families. But a lot of them send their kids to Providence-St. Mel [Pharoah's school]. Most of them are good kids.

Some kids who are at Providence-St. Mel are on scholarship. They've been going to schools in public housing, like Souter or Henry Horner. At Providence-St. Mel, they try to see if people who, if they had a chance, can do well. So they give these kids a chance, but sometimes they're bad kids because they come from the projects and stuff.

Do you think if the kids at Henry Horner had a chance to go to a good school, or otherwise to get out, do you think they would do well? I don't really know because some of them can't even read; they're illiterate. We just gotta start at a young age, to start them liking school.

There was just something in me—I just liked school as a kid. I don't know why; I just did. When my big brother Laffie used to go to school, when I was little, my mother told me I used to always go and put on my clothes and get ready with Laffie, and pretend like I was going to school. I'd put a lot of tissue in a bag and pretend like it was a book bag.

Now I like school less; I don't know why. But I would never drop out. If I drop out, I'll be part of the problem—not part of the solution, because I won't be helping anybody. Plus I'll make my mama feel even worse than she already feels because I'm going to be the only person [in the family] to go on to college. And that will really make her happy.

Do you think you could be president someday if you wanted to be? I don't know about that. I have to know a lot more about the issues. Plus with race nowadays . . . I don't think there will be a black president in my time. I just don't. I hope so, but there's a lot of prejudice around. Some blacks are capable of running as president. But like Jesse Jackson, he made a big mistake in New York, when he said something bad about Jews. He was trying to be funny, but he wasn't funny. That really hurt him. He was doing real good before that. That was really dumb on his part. Why'd he need to say that? He just wasn't thinking.

Since 1978, principal Paul Adams has run Providence-St. Mel as a private institution for 500 African-American students. Adams has strict rules—no drugs, no gangs, no excessive absences or tardiness—and rewards students financially for making the honor roll. After graduation, over 90 percent go on to college.

Around the projects during the last election time [in 1988], if you asked people who's running for president, they'd say Jesse Jackson. That's the only person they know. But now when I ask my friends who is running for president, they don't even know.

Would they be more interested if there were a black candidate? Yeah, I think so. They should also tell candidates that a lot of the black people in poor communities, like Henry Horner and Rockwell, are ready for a change too. This election [in 1992] there was a record number of voters in the black community. So that shows they're ready for a change.

*D*o you think racism is a bad problem? Yes. I haven't really had bad experiences that hit home, but sometimes I really know a person is racist. I'll get on the bus, and as soon as I sit down, they'll move. I don't know if they're afraid of me. Maybe they've just never had contact with a black person.

I don't think there's anything we can do about racism, really. It's just up to the people. They've got to get to know other people. They've got to get to know someone besides their own color and race. Then, they can make a judgment. Just because one black is bad, it doesn't mean that all blacks are bad. Just because one white is bad doesn't mean that all of them are bad.

I have a lot of white friends. I think racism is less around people my age, because we mix up more and get to know each other.

*D*o you think you're affected by things that the government does? Not really. [*Pause*] Do you mean like how much money they're spending on different programs? No, I don't really think I'm affected by the government.

I think now the government is paying a little bit more attention to places like Henry Horner. They don't like to have these places all ugly, so they're cleaning it up. But that's the easy part: cleaning it up. The hard part is making it a safe community where people will want to invest their money. They're 25 percent of the way there now. [*Chuckles*] It's a start.

*H*ow would you describe a good citizen? I think a good citizen of the country does something for American society. Like becoming a judge. Or some way helping out our society or the economy.

I think a good citizen would vote. And volunteer to help their communities. That's better than always looking for material things. They could do something spiritually and from the heart. Like helping out to keep the place clean, volunteering to answer calls, just little bitty things that add up.

I'm going to vote when I get old enough. I think it's important to vote. But I think the voting age should be lowered to like fifteen or something like that because most kids who are fifteen know what they're talking about. And that's our future. I think we should have a choice in our future.

*D*o you think the government's doing a good job? I think it's doing an okay job, not good enough. Because they've just now started paying attention to places like Henry Horner. I think they should do more recreational things for kids, like a corner hangout, like the Boys Club, or the Y, something like that.

*D*o you know about some of the laws the government makes that are supposed to make life better for people? I think that passing a bill is only the first step. When a bill is passed, that's only a small number of people who happen to be in the Congress. I'm not saying that everybody should be able to vote on a bill. But like when they passed the civil rights bill, blacks were able to vote but they still didn't get equal rights. Like when they went to vote, they got whipped and beat because they were voting. So just because you pass a law, it doesn't mean that you've solved the problem.

*A*re you familiar with types of government in other countries? Not too much, but a little bit. I know that Canada is thinking about breaking up, right? I read in the paper that they had a vote to break up.

*W*ell, the French Canadians in Quebec feel like a minority in someone else's country, and some would like to have their own, separate country. Just think about if everybody wanted to do that. All blacks wanted to go to their own state, all Baptists in one state, all Jewish people in one state. I think that's a bad thing.

Why do they think of themselves as a minority? I don't really like the term "minority" used like for Hispanics in the United States because doesn't "minority" mean, like, lower than?

*L*iterally it just means smaller in number, fewer people. *But you think it means lower than?* Yeah. Yeah, I think so.

*D*o you think you'd like to live anywhere other than the United States? No. But I know that there are a lot of countries safer than we are.

*W*hat do you like the best about living in this country? Freedom of speech. Being free to express yourself. Being independent. You have a lot of freedom here, as opposed to other countries. So I like that.

*W*hat do you think of politicians? Do you trust them? It all depends. I think politicians say anything to get elected. Some politicians are crooked. They bounce checks and things like that. And they think they can get away with it.

Some are good. Like that man with the dotted tie—Paul Simon. Outside of Illinois: Mario Cuomo. That's basically it. Bill Clinton, maybe, but I don't really know. He just started. He sounds good. Also, Jack Kemp. He's not that conservative. He's a little liberal. He's really in between. I like that. He helps people who are trying to help themselves.

*W*hat do you think the "American dream" means? Like you grow up to be independent, working, have children. The American dream is for every kid to grow up and not worry about the kind of clothes they wear, that they won't get taken off their body. For every kid to go on to college and make something of their lives. No drugs in their society. Just a safe, clean environment.

My American dream is to grow up, have kids, a nice family, be working independently, be a businessman, maybe think of becoming a Congressman or something like that.

***W**hat do you think the country will be like in fifty years?* I don't know, really. I think it'll be a better place, because we're making some changes. A Democratic president in office. They're starting to do more things to shake up the economy. Cleaning up Henry Horner. More police on the street. Things like that. It's a start for things bigger.

What makes people different? Their abilities in volleyball and karate? Their love of helping other people? Their way of speaking with their hands? Cynthia Hunt, a seventeen-year-old high school student, has all of those characteristics and more. However, she thinks there is one that tends to define her more than it should: she can't hear. Deaf since an early age, Cynthia and her parents have never let deafness become an excuse for opting out of anything. So today, the Gallaudet Model Secondary School for the Deaf (MSSD) junior feels there is nothing she can't do, from traveling to building a shelf in her room, from peer counseling to teaching English to the deaf. She, as do other deaf people, communicates just as vibrantly and perhaps more vividly than "hearies" by using her hands, facial expressions, and body language. At her core, she's just an American teenager with a free-wheeling sense of humor and a love of adventure who wants others to treat her and all deaf people with the same respect they would anybody else.

*M*any hearing people don't really understand what it's like being deaf. Can you tell me what it's like? What does it feel like to be deaf? I don't know what it feels like to be hearing! The feeling is just the same as you feel about being hearing. It's the way I was made.

With music, I *see* it, even though it's nothing but sound. I feel I can visualize it through the vibrations, while you hear it. One way I feel sorry for hearing people is that they hear *a lot* of noises, while I can't. So, I am thankful for that!

There are different levels of deafness. I am profoundly deaf, but I have been using hearing aids in both ears since I was about four years old. I had to turn up the volume to the max, but I still couldn't hear. When I was thirteen, I fell and hit my head on the floor. After that, my right ear started to improve a little bit. And my mother said, "What happened? Did something fall out of your ear?" I just didn't know. Ever since then, I just use the hearing aid in my right ear. I can hear, but my audiogram still shows that I am profoundly deaf without my hearing aid.

*S*o can you hear me a little bit? No. I shut off my hearing aid. [*Smiling*] I got tired of hearing all the noises of all those people screaming! The nice thing about being deaf is when I use the hearing aid, if there is screaming, I just turn it off, and I can't hear anymore. [*Editor's note: Most deaf people are not voice-impaired, and they often use vocal sounds with their signing. There can be a lot of noise at a school with deaf students!*]

I've read that there is some controversy about the proper language for deaf people to use: American Sign Language (ASL), or Signed Exact English (SEE), or something else. Why there is a controversy? I don't understand that part myself, because they are both sign language, period, you know? The deaf people have labeled ASL as their language, just like the Chinese have their own language. ASL is an abbreviation of sentences in signs. Like "I go store." That's how they would write it. While in proper English, they would say, "I'm going to the store," in that word order. ASL has some signs that can mean another word than what they are really trying to say. I guess the feeling is that

ASL is more of the way that they speak. Right now, I'm using PSE. Pidgin Signed English. It's not really SEE and it's not really ASL. It's in-between.

There have been some friends of mine who sign only ASL and don't have the good English skills. So it was a little difficult for them to understand me. I had to change to completely ASL. You just have to know their capabilities. That's why I am glad that I know how to change things around. I want to be an English teacher because I've seen some kids that have a difficult time trying to tell the difference between ASL and written English. There are some kids that can only picture things in their head, which is fine with me, just as long as they know how to write it in the proper English structure.

I want to be the one that teaches them. They need good English skills to get along in life. Hearing people are set on one [way of communicating], and deaf people have two [written English and ASL]. That's why I want to become an English teacher. I am going to find a way to teach them. I don't know yet how, but I am going to do it.

If you had the chance today to have all your hearing back, would you want it?
My mom asked me the same question many times: "If they invented a pill that could make you hearing again, what would you do? Would you take it?" I said, "No! Because I am proud of who I am today." I mean, if you don't like me, that's your loss, because you don't know me. If they like me, fine, that's great. I don't feel I need to change anything because I like who I am.

There are some deaf people out there who are very involved with the deaf culture—more than I am. I am more of an in-between. I feel like I'm a bridge between the hearing and the deaf world since I have hearing parents and hearing relatives—they're all hearing except for me. I have hearing friends, and whoever I talk with almost always is hearing.

Some deaf people refuse to talk to any hearing people—they don't feel comfortable being with them. They are very "deaf" in their thinking, not just physically, but mentally, very "deaf." They just shut out anything related to hearing people.

Maybe [it's similar to the way] some black people are against white people—because they have been racially discriminated against for a very long time. The hearing people have discriminated against the deaf people for a long time. Now, there is starting to be more under-standing about deaf people. But I guess deaf people are just starting to feel, "Hey, I want my world." They are very outspoken sometimes, and I think that is good, but sometimes I don't think that's good. Because they [hearing people] are starting to accept us, that's fine—accept them. I don't see any reasons why we can't accept each other!

I don't see a lot of discrimination, but some deaf people out there tell me, yeah, there is a lot of discrimination. When I look at it my way, I don't see it as discrimination against us. There are some hearing peo-ple who are afraid of us, who don't know how to communicate with us. There is a fear inside of them.

A friend of mine who is hearing was a lifeguard at my pool when he first met me—and he was scared to death about me! He didn't know how to communicate with me. He had never seen a deaf person before; he never knew what to do. So I tried to help him understand that there is nothing wrong with me—I just can't hear. And he learned sign language, and we've been good friends ever since.

*D*o you think there are equal opportunities in work? It might be a little more difficult for us, being deaf, to get jobs than it would be for a hearing person to get a job. I guess we have to get them to hire an interpreter for the job interview and they probably wouldn't want to waste the money for that.

With the ADA [Americans with Disabilities Act, 1990] that has been passed, there should be more equal opportunities for us to get jobs. There are a lot of deaf people out there that they just can't reject. I mean, it's just like being black and white. Do they have equal job opportunities for black and white? Back then they didn't, but now they do. So it's the same thing with hearing and deaf people.

*D*o you think the ADA is successful? Pretty good so far. I went into a restaurant that happened to have a bar, and it had a TV. And I saw that the TV had captioning [readable captions] included. So it was good. At my mom's job, they finally started to hire interpreters instead of using her as an interpreter. And that's good to know that deaf people can be hired out there.

How do you think we can change the attitudes of individuals about deaf people? It will probably take a lot of effort, but it is possible. We'll probably need to let people know that we, as deaf people, won't bite!

The Americans with Disabilities Act (ADA) was passed by Congress in 1990. The law prohibits discrimination against people with physical and mental impairments in employment, transportation, telecommunications, services, and public accommodations such as restaurants, theaters, and stores.

We're not animals, you know, we're humans—we just can't hear. We can do anything that they want us to do. We're smart; we're exactly like them. We need to understand that the hearing people won't bite us either. Not everyone is hearing-discriminatory. We just have to look out for the ones that do accept us. And for the ones that don't, we just need to reach out and touch them. Send out some messages on things like this.

Public appearances could work pretty well. Like, for example, Marlee Matlin in "Unreasonable Doubts." Look, she's doing a TV show. She has a main character. That shows that deaf people can do anything that hearing people want to do. Maybe a program for people that don't understand each other, or a workshop or something like that. Maybe a book on it. I don't know. Maybe I'll be the one who writes the book!

It sounds like your parents have a big role in your life—how have they influenced you? In a lot of ways they have. My mom made me grow into a strong person because she is a strong person herself. She believes in believing in what she believes in. She won't let other people change her. What she says is it—she stays with it. She taught me that.

My father taught me to not be a quitter. There were times when I wanted to quit a sport, and my dad would say, "No, stay, you can do it." "Practice makes perfect"—that's his philosophy. My dad also wanted me to be a teacher—he is a teacher himself—so I guess that is where I get the idea of being a teacher.

They also just taught me how to be a very thoughtful person, to take care of other people, not to think of myself only. My mom and I are the same. When they [other people] have problems, we'll take care of it for them, make sure that they are alright. We always put our problems last until there is nothing left. But I guess that's good, if I want to be a thoughtful, caring person!

They both have really made me who I am today. They taught me that I should always remember that I can do whatever I want to do—not I can't because I am deaf. When they ask me to do something, I say, "No, I can't do that." They'll say, "Well, why not?" And I'll just say, "Because I am deaf." My mom and dad say, "No, you don't have that excuse." When I see other people using that excuse, it makes me feel that they are trying to put themselves down, and trying to make us, the deaf people, look bad. When a hearing person sees a deaf person say, "No, I can't do that; I can't hear," often that person will think that *no* other deaf people can. That becomes the way they view the whole deaf community.

*W*e've talked about discrimination between hearing and deaf people. What about racial discrimination? How do you think the country is doing in overcoming that? There is still a lot of racial discrimination going on out there, whether we like it or not. It may come from inside a person, or out in the public. But I don't think racial discrimination is necessary because anybody of whatever race, color, sex, or anything is a human being, just like us. They might have their own culture, like the black people have their own culture, the white people have their own culture—there is nothing wrong with that. That's why I feel a little sick when I see racial discrimination, because I feel that people should be given equal opportunities.

I feel sorry for the victims of racial discrimination, because I know how it is to be discriminated against. I just wish that I could tell everybody, "Hey, you know, stop discriminating, it's unnecessary." But I know that I can't do that because one person can't really do all of the work. If I could get a lot of people together that thought like I did, then maybe, just maybe, we could get the message across.

I feel very strongly against racial discrimination. I have a lot of friends who are different from me. They might be mentally retarded; they might be physically handicapped; they might be black, orange, red, yellow, whatever. I don't care. I love them just the same.

So on this, and other issues, do you feel that you can make a difference? I could, yeah [*nodding*]. If people would listen to me. For example, on discrimination against homosexuals, one of my teachers made a remark against gay people. I was very upset with that. Some people don't feel very comfortable with them, and that's fine. I don't feel comfortable with them doing things in front of me, no, but I respect their feelings, their personal choice. I tried to get my teacher to look on their side. And he refused to listen. So the second day I tried to discuss this with him again. He wasn't too up for it, but he was trying to change for my sake. And I told him, "I'm still going to work on it." If I can get him to change, then maybe I can make some other people change if they are willing to listen to me instead of arguing with me. There aren't too many people out there that are willing to listen to any side except their own.

You say one of the things that you value doing is helping others. Could you tell me a couple of ways that you do that? Help others by letting them know that I accept them for who they are and that I love them, no matter what they do. If they do something wrong, I'll accept that, just as long as they learn from their mistakes. I have several friends in the school that are physically handicapped or that can't really communicate with other people. I am a senior peer adviser for that group [physically and mentally disabled students]. So I try to reach out and touch them. Maybe not in too many words, but actions really show more than just saying it. Let them know that there are people like me out there that do care about them.

There are students here who are really, really awful to them. And I feel, you know, "Come on, why are you picking on them? They can't defend themselves. They are just letting it happen." They're as much a victim as we are in the real world, because the hearing people might oppress us.

*W*hat is your definition of a good citizen? A good citizen who has a perfect record? That would be pretty hard to do! [*Smiling*] A good citizen is someone who gets involved with programs, like, let's say the DARE programs—teaching other people to be good citizens and not to use drugs because they can hurt them or other people. A good citizen also understands the government and how it works, even though they might not accept what it is trying to do, but, you know, working with them, instead of going out there and setting up a protest or riots or anything like that. A good citizen works with people instead of against them.

I don't think they have to be smart or anything like that; they can be anyone. Black, red, white, deaf, hearing, mentally retarded, physically handicapped people. I mean *anyone*.

*S*ometimes people your age are criticized for not caring about what is going on in the country or the government. Do you think that is valid? No! There are some kids my age that really don't give a damn about the government and what's going on out there, that's true, yes. But there are some other kids that really do care. They listen to the radio, or they are watching the news, or they're reading the newspaper every day. Me, for one, I do care. It's just that I don't have time to always pick up a newspaper and spend the time to read it with the busy schedule that I have.

The problem is with the TV—I just turned on the news yesterday, and I was trying to find a news station that was captioned, because I can't understand what's going on without captioning. So I flipped the channel, flipped the channel, and there was no news that was captioned. How do you expect us deaf people to understand what's going on out there? At eleven o'clock—that's about my bedtime right now—I had to go to sleep, and I missed the news that is captioned. I think it should be switched; show most captioned news around six o'clock or news time.

I also talk with my parents about what's going on. After that, I find out what is going on through teachers and friends. It's not true that teenagers my age don't care. They do care; it's just that in their own way they do.

For the next presidential election, I will vote. In my opinion, I think that if you want to be a true, loyal citizen to America, then you should vote for who you really believe would do a good job. Not just sit back and let it happen. One voter could make a big difference. Most

people don't think that—that's what causes the high percentage of people not voting. What if the whole nation ended up not even voting at all? I mean, who would be our next president? They need to understand that they will make a difference, no matter what.

What did you think of the presidential election? Pretty competitive. It was a hard choice because each presidential candidate has their own faults, and each has their plans that they say they are going to do, but will they really do it? Like for example, in the last presidential election [in 1988] Bush said, "Read my lips, no new taxes." But look at him [*exasperated*]. He created new taxes. But there is no one that we can really trust anyway. We just need to have someone in charge of this nation. I had a little more stronger feelings this time for Clinton, because I wanted to have somebody new, a new party. I got sick and tired of the Republican party. I'm not a Republican, I'm more of a Democrat, and that's why. I felt that they had some pretty good suggestions for plans to change the economy and to improve America.

To bring us out of the darkness. Bush, on the other hand, was okay, but he was a little unstable. He said he would change, but would he? Who knows? I guess we'll never find out.

Do you trust politicians? Yes and no. They can be very cunning, very slick, getting what they want, but there are some politicians that really do care about us, about what we need, about our health, our welfare, and all of that. There are some politicians that are just in it for the money or something like that.

> **The word 'impaired' means broken, something to fix. We have nothing to fix. We feel normal because we were born this way. There's nothing to fix.**
>
> Janet Weinstock, a deaf history teacher at MSSD, as quoted in the *Washington City Paper*, May 29-June 4, 1992

Would you ever run for political office yourself? No, because of the fear that whatever I am trying to propose to Congress, they would reject, or give me a hard time. I wouldn't get what I wanted passed. Too much of a hassle! I would rather stand by and be a loyal citizen and have my own beliefs and do what I can do in the community, rather than being in a stuffy old building trying to debate about getting something that I want passed.

Where have you learned what you know about government? American government class, first semester. To be truthful, I didn't know anything about the government and the way it works until this class that I took. I learned a lot of things through that class.

Which right from the Constitution do you treasure the most? As a student, the right to privacy. If somebody barges into my room and says, "There are some kids out there who are using drugs and I think you are one of them, so I want to go through your room," I can say,

"Hey, wait a minute, I don't use drugs, and I don't have anything in my room." Just because I am a student and live here doesn't mean that they can be my parent and just barge into my room without a warrant. If they do really suspect me, then fine. But if they don't have any strong evidence, then they cannot do that to us. That is an invasion of privacy.

And I do value the freedom of speech. If we can't say anything that we want to say, then there could be a lot problems.

*W*hat do you think your responsibilities are as an American? My responsibility as an American is to help other people and to make sure that they don't go into the wrong things. I don't want to see anyone get hurt, or hurt other people, whether it be alcohol or drugs, or any of those other kinds of abuses. And to protect anyone's rights, because they have their own rights. Black people, deaf people, females all have their own rights. I want to make sure that the minority knows that, and that they can defend themselves if it comes to [that]. That's what I feel like my responsibilities are as an American. And to be a really loyal American.

*H*ave you traveled to other countries? No, but I would like to. I plan to some day.

*D*o you know anything about other forms of government? Yes, communism that used to exist in Russia. That's why I'm glad it's not there anymore, even though there are still, I'm sure, some people in there that are communists. You know, some people just can't change overnight. I also understand that there are some countries that are still in turmoil and confusion, because they don't have any form of government. And that's sad because in confusion, nobody knows what to do.

*S*o if you had the option of living anywhere in the world that you wanted, where would it be? That's a good question. There are a lot of places that I would like to be in, but . . . a good place to live? [*Pause*] That's hard. I guess England. Because they speak a similar language to us, so I wouldn't have to go through the classes to learn a new language. I feel that they're more organized than most of the other countries. And [*teasingly*] there are a lot of juicy little rumors going on there that I would like to hear the full stories about! Russia, yeah, but the economy there is not too good. So I don't want to live through those hard times. And any country that still has communism, no way, I don't want to live there.

But of all the countries of the world, I would rather live here in America. Because it's my home, it's who I am. I grew up here. I have the same values, the same morals as American people. I feel that, you know, we're the same, and we have more choices of who we want to be, like who is going to be in charge of America, such as the Democrats, Republicans, or whatever party. We have more freedoms here. I like the spice that America provides.

What do you think is the biggest problem facing America right now? Unemployment. There are lots and lots of people that have been laid off in the past four years. That really worries me because there are more and more people becoming homeless because they can't afford to keep up their house payments or pay off their bills. That's just too many people living on the street. When the wintertime comes, they're cold, they're laying on the street, there is no food. You know, I feel bad for those people. That is one of the biggest problems.

What causes that problem is the economy part. Businesses don't have the money to keep people on their payrolls. The budgets are cut, so they don't have any choices but to cut off their workers too, put them out onto the streets. That's what I think is one of the biggest problems in this country.

How do you think we can solve it? Be a little more reasonable on what we spend. I read in one newspaper where we were planning to spend something like $27 billion on a few airplanes—"airtoys" that we really don't need. That is a waste of money! That money could go to some other really good cause. We're too busy competing on weapons, you know—who can kill the best. I mean, come on!

What do you think America will be like in fifty years? It depends on who is our president. It's really hard to tell because it seems that we keep going up and down, up and down, up and down. So it's really hard to predict. In fifty years, we could be one of the richest countries in the world again. Or we could be one of the poorest countries in the world. A lot of things could happen.

In the past four years, I could see things going downhill. But now with Clinton, I am hoping that it will go back up again. The last I heard this morning, in the newspaper, I heard that we were going up. It's getting a little better, so there is some hope for us.

What's great about America? The variety of people in America. The physical capabilities, the mental capabilities, the races, the sexes. What's great is that we can really mix. At this school [MSSD], students come from almost every state, and they mix up here. And that's what I like. I don't like just one group. I mean, it would be boring, you know? To see the same thing everyday. But here, you get more spice in life, you meet different kinds of people, from different countries. That's what I like most about America.

Who is your hero? There is somebody that I do consider my hero, and that's God, because without him, I don't know how I would get along in life. I mean, when I have problems, I always turn to God and he always seems to help me out! Some people don't even believe in him, and I don't understand why because it is a proven fact in the Bible that he does exist, period. So I guess that is my hero— God.

What's your American dream? Mine would be to have no racial discrimination, no sexual discrimination, no discrimination against hearing or deaf people. Of course, the country would have flaws, but I just want to see everyone happy. That's my dream, to see everyone happy. And not so against each other, or so much violence or crime because they are not happy and all that.

*A*nd what about just for you? That's hard to think of only myself. I want to travel, maybe to different deaf schools and see what they are doing. Help other English teachers teach the kids the difference between ASL and English. I would just like to have a very successful life, doing what I.like doing, helping other people become successful in their lives. That is my dream, to see other people be successful. By making them successful, that would make me successful too, because I know that I have accomplished something, not just for me, but for them too.

Editor's note: Cynthia and I spoke through an interpreter, Deb Tomardy, courtesy of Gallaudet's Public Relations Department.

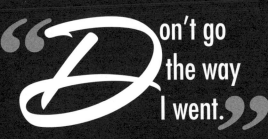

"**D**on't go
the way
I went."

Katherine J. Olson

After fleeing from uncaring parents and
an "ordinary" life, Katherine Olson, then
a petite thirteen-year-old with piercing
blue eyes, did what she felt was necessary to survive on the streets. Kat
linked up with a Jamaican boyfriend and
entered the big-time drug trade in
Baltimore, Maryland. Kat loved the
excitement of "gangster" life and the
challenge of standing on equal footing in
a market dominated by black male teens.
But the downside of the business—gun-
fights, watching friends die, killing people—finally got to her. Two narcotics
officers helped bring her off the street
and into the Fellowship of Lights, a shelter for runaway and homeless teens.
There, seventeen-year-old Kat, though
weary-eyed, smiles and laughs easily
when talking about her brutal experiences on the street, as if they were all a
dream. Now she's taking her first small
steps toward turning from a hardened
street criminal into a compassionate and
productive member of her community.

How did you end up on the streets? Me and my parents never got along anyways. Me and my stepfather hated each other, and my mom would choose him over her children. He already chased away my older sister. Then we had our final blowout when I was thirteen over me going with black guys and stuff. It was a mixture of them kicking me out and me leaving. I went to live with my boyfriend, and my parents moved back to Texas. Then me and my boyfriend broke up, so I started dealing drugs and working for other people.

I started using drugs when I was about fifteen or sixteen. Before that I was using pot. My boyfriend was Jamaican and smoked a lot. At first I was like, "No," but then I started smoking pot. Then from pot I started snorting heroin once in a while. Then from heroin I started using ready rock and snorting coke—but I was like a social user. I didn't use it all the time. I just did it when I wanted to.

I know drugs are bad for you. But what really gets me was, in school, I wouldn't do that good on tests, but when I snorted coke and I would take my tests, I always got good grades. I could never figure it out! [*Laughing*]

You could get a vial of cocaine that already had the scooper in it for like $800. One would last me for about two weeks. I'd carry that around with me in school, and I'd go in the bathroom and take two hits in each nose and go back out there and be fine. I even did LSD in school twice [*proudly*]. The last time I used drugs was about four months ago.

Do you think you are off them for good? Probably, yeah.

Why did you drop out of school? I couldn't pay attention in regular schools. The work in regular schools was too hard, and I just couldn't understand what they were doing. I was in a special education school, and I was getting As in every class but English, where I was getting Ds. There, a class consists of one to five people. That was more interesting; the teachers helped you.

But also, I'd be up all night selling, and I didn't have enough time for school work. I'd come to school and would be too tired to even pay attention. I dropped out in December of '92. I was in eleventh grade.

When I was living with my parents, I used to sell drugs out of the house. People would come and they'd throw something at my window. I had a basket that I had tied a rope onto. I would lower the basket down and they would put maybe $20 or $40 in it. If they wanted a bag of pot, I would weigh it out on my scale and then I would put it in the basket and that was that. But then the cops started watching the house, so I was like, "I can't do this no more. If this house gets raided, my parents are going to *kill* me."

After my parents left, I first started selling on street corners. That's when you learn how to hustle. I would stand on the street corner and cars would go by. If they wanted something, they would circle around three or four times. Finally they would stop and they'd say, "What's up?" and I'd say, "What's up?" and they'd say, "What's going on?" I'd say, "What do you want?" and they would tell me and I would say if I had it or not. I would make maybe $500 a week.

I've been doing it since I was thirteen. Basically it's the only job I know how to do and I'm good at. I'm an excellent hustler. [*Smiling*] I know a lot about drugs. I can sell them good and I can make them. I sold heroin, which is called joint or smack or big J. I've sold pot, which is called reefer. I've sold PCP, LSD, and Sherman sticks, which are cigarettes dipped in LSD. For a little while I was selling ready rock and crack. Ready rock is regular cocaine cooked in baking soda and water, and crack is cooked in baking soda and ammonia. I have sold everything . . . everything! [*Laughs*]

When I was fourteen, I met my boyfriend, my baby's father, and we started saving our money and in two months, we started our own organization. I had even taken in two homeless boys. One guy was working for other people, and he wasn't making nothing but like $10 a day. So I brought him in, let him start working for us. Within two weeks they had their own apartments, their own cars, and beepers and stuff.

We had eight people working for us. All the people that were working for us were making anywhere from $1000 to maybe $2000 a week. Between me and my boyfriend, we'd bring in $10,000 a week. I had my own car. I had a beeper and nice clothes—you never saw me wear the same outfit twice within a year.

I spent my money on rent, electricity, beeper activation, and car insurance. Of course, the car wasn't in my name because I don't even have a license! We would also spend money on trips and packages. There would be a lot of times we would go up to New York and we'd buy kilos and stuff.

*D*id you ever get busted? Very close to being busted many times. We were coming back from Florida one time. We were at the airport and we had ten kilos—everything in bags of coffee so dogs can't pick up the scent. For some reason, though, the dogs they had in the airport started going crazy around our bags, so we thought, "We're busted now." But it wasn't our bag; it was another person's bag that had pot in it.

Many times we were sitting in the house and we all came very close to being busted. We woke up one morning and we both had a funny feeling that the house was going to get raided that night, so we took our money and left. And that same night my boyfriend's brother had gone over to the house. We went to pick him up and there were cops everywhere. He got busted with a .25 caliber, drugs, and lots of money. He is still in jail because his bail is $25,000, and I don't think he's getting out. He's going to get anywhere from three to five years in jail.

*D*id those close calls ever make you think about getting out of it? Now it does, yeah, but before, no, because I was . . . I was always slick about everything, really. We always kept everything by the toilets—no matter how much we had. When we'd go to these houses, we'd carry $20 on us, but by the time we'd finish selling, we'd have lots. If we made a grand, one of us would take it to the house to get it in the safe. But I know sooner or later I would have gotten busted.

It was the adventure, the excitement, the money, the danger. It was pretty much all of them. I was tired of being one of them ordinary kids, doing nothing. I wanted to be a gangster, so I got in the gangster lifestyle.

You had been carrying a gun since you were thirteen? Yes. When you are in the drug dealing business and you work for Jamaicans, you always have your way of getting guns, no matter where you're at. The guy I started working for was like, "You're white, you're small—you're going to need protection!" and he just pulled out all these guns and said, "Take your choice." The .22 was too small—it wouldn't really do that much damage, but the .25 was easy for me to handle, easy to shoot, and it had hollow point bullets so when it hit somebody, it ricocheted in the body and it would do damage. So that's why I got that.

One time, me and my boyfriend were standing in front of O'Dell's after it closed, and there were two people standing next to us in a crowd. Then, these people started going by and my boyfriend was like, "Get on the ground!" He threw me on the ground and he was on top of me. Then I heard these gun shots. He was laying on me, shooting his gun, and I'm underneath him shooting my gun. The two people next to me had gotten their heads blown off. All my clothes were soaked in blood; my hair was drenched in blood. More than likely it was drugs.

I've gotten shot once. It was a big gun fight and I got shot in my right leg with a nine millimeter and I was so mad, I didn't really feel it. Then a couple of hours later I finally went to the hospital. They had called the cops since I was a juvenile and it was a gunshot wound, but luckily for me they had already taken out the bullet and wrapped it up and stuff. I just took off.

For everybody, I think, the first time they shoot somebody, they are shocked. I remember my first time, I was just like, "Oh my gosh, I can't believe I did this, no way!" I was down to tears. I didn't even really want to do it, but I was ordered to. Then after that, I could shoot somebody and wouldn't even care. I would just think it was their own fault. But sometimes innocent bystanders would get clipped or shot, and then I would feel bad about it.

There's a lot of times I feel like, "I can't believe I'm selling drugs, I can't believe I'm shooting people," but then a lot of times it would be like, "Well, I've got to do it to survive." If nobody likes it, you know, that's their problem. I had food, I had a roof over my head, clothes, a car. At times I didn't really think about it or care; it was just what I got to do.

*W*hat do you think of the gang scene in Los Angeles? Well, my sister's fiancé is a member of the Bloods in L.A. They're *scary*—but they are a lot of fun. But South Central L.A., that even scares *me!* When I went there, I walked with my gun showing, I didn't care that it was illegal— that's how scared I was. And I ain't never going back if I can help it.

*H*ow did you end up in Fellowship of Lights? I ended up joining the Fellowship of Lights because I had gotten really bad into dealing drugs. I was working out of this house where four Jamaicans were dealing out of. One night, me and my best friend John and this other guy were talking to friends through a bedroom window when this guy named Marky called John over. Then I saw Marky shoot John. He knew I saw it. Somehow the police also found out that I saw it, and they were tracking me down. When they came to my house two days later looking for me, the people in the house thought I told the police.

When I went back, the Jamaicans beat me up. I got two guns held to my head. I was beaten with a broken broomstick, punched, kicked, hit by the handle of the guns. One of the guys had taken a knife and was hitting me all over with it. I had been thrown from one side of the room to the other. I was like a punching bag.

I don't know why they didn't kill me. I never figured that one out. I jumped out of the top story bedroom window and ran to my boyfriend's best friend's house. I called homicide the next day and decided to tell them everything that happened.

The next thing you know, I was helping the narcotics police. They wanted to bust the house I was working out of. We did surveillance on the house looking for Marky for like three days. Finally an officer went to this liquor store because he does duty there, and sure enough there's Marky coming out of the liquor store. I did a positive identification. He is in jail now for murder one.

I kept on helping these narcotics officers bust people by tipping them off with information. But then one of the guys that had gotten locked up got out of jail and came to my apartment. He held a gun to my head and was saying, "You're a snitch, you're Five-O, you called the cops, you got me busted!" So I ran and called the narcotics officers and asked them to come pick me up.

> The Fellowship of Lights is a 21-year-old nonprofit shelter for youth, in Baltimore, Maryland, and part of the United Way national network. Kids usually come in homeless, as runaways, or as unsuccessful foster home placements.

Finally, I pressed charges on him, and they found him with a big, long knife and he told them—these were his exact words—"I want to find that bitch and cut her up in little pieces." So they arrested him for possession of illegal weapons and assault. He told a lot of people that I was a snitch, though, and they believed it. It wasn't safe for me to go back there anymore, so they put me in the Fellowship of Lights. I've been there ever since.

How do you feel about being pregnant at seventeen? I'm happy about it! This is my second pregnancy. First one I had a stillborn. I really couldn't give a squat what other people think about it. I know a lot of people say, "Your baby is going to be racially mixed; it's going to have a hard time growing up."

I told them I don't care. If anybody touches my daughter or my son, they are going to have to deal with me—and if they knew about me back when I was younger, they won't want to mess with me or my child.

I can't wait till I have my baby. People might think it's bad to be a single mom, but it will probably be easier than having two parents. It will be my child. I won't have somebody telling me what to do.

I want lots of kids. Of course I want a father for them later on. I don't want to be a single parent to six kids! For now, it's already too expensive for one kid, but I will do everything to give my child the best life he or she could have.

I just have always loved kids. Even when I was younger I loved them, and I was still one myself! I think it's because I know they like me and they know I like them and I like teaching them, helping them. I like experiencing stuff with them.

> I'd like to think that this is a turning point for Kat. When she first came here, she said her goal was 'to live through the day.' Now, she's talking about getting her G.E.D. [General Educational Development diploma] and going into police work.
>
> Mary Lou Hobbs, Counselor, Fellowship of Lights

I'll be a good mother, I know that much. If I caught my child doing drugs, I'd beat the heck out of it and throw it into rehab. Then he really would regret me being his mother! [*Laughter*] You know, if they did drugs, I would still love them, but I would make sure they got help for it and they didn't do it no more.

I would take it places. I will do everything I can so it won't sell drugs. If I had to, I'd work three jobs just so it could have money to get what it wanted; then it wouldn't turn to selling drugs. If I had a boy and he wanted to go with a white girl or a black girl, I would still approve of it. I'm not going to be racial like my family is and disown him.

My parents think all the choices I've made are stupid, ignorant, childish, immature, and everything. To me, my choices were pretty smart—I'm still living. I don't care what they think. They really don't know all that I've been through. They're like, "Well, that's your stupid fault." Well, it wouldn't be my fault if they would have kept me, so they can't blame everything on me.

I don't feel like I am seventeen; I feel like I'm twenty-something. I feel like I'm almost old. A lot of people say I matured in a hard way, but to me it was for my own good because if I wouldn't have grown up like that, I would probably be lost in the world right now. I'd probably still be with my parents taking their little abusive ways.

Your life is very different from that of most teens. What would you tell them about this lifestyle? Don't go the way I went! It may be fun, exciting, dangerous, and all that, but a lot of my friends didn't make it. Me and my best friend are the only—I guess you could say survivors. Everybody else is dead. I would tell them to stay in high school, get your education, get a legal job. Don't even think about it; it's not a lifestyle. It was a matter of time before I would have been killed or busted. I would—not to be rude—but especially for a white person, I would really tell them don't go this way.

Why especially for a white person? Because a lot of black people deal. I was the only white girl selling; there wasn't even a white boy nowhere. Even in the city, the only white people that you did see weren't really selling. They were coke fiends. They would just do it so they could get the drugs. But I did it because I got money for it.

At one point I had a real big problem with racism because I was white and most drug dealers and other people were black. They were scared to buy from a white person because they thought all white people were narcs. They would always discriminate against me by not buying from me, making slurred comments to me, shooting at me.

I would say it is a problem. Racism is the one thing you can't get around; you have to deal with it one way or another.

I remember when I was fourteen, I was walking through the mall with my boyfriend, who was black, and people didn't think it was right. We had gone in the store to get a card for his mother's birthday and the lady wouldn't sell it to us. She told us we had to leave. I was about to pull out my gun and shoot her, I was so mad. It was hard for us to do anything. We couldn't even go eat at a restaurant. But times have changed now.

*W*hat did you think of the L.A. riots? Personally, I didn't think it was right what they did to Rodney King. I found it very discriminating. Even though it all happened up there, I think everywhere, blacks were very mad about it and blacks were going fighting against whites and stuff. I found it very hard to believe that people in our society would be like that, especially cops. I found it disgusting towards my race, actually.

Even my boyfriend was disgusted. There was a point where he was so mad at white people, he wouldn't even talk to me, and I was like, "I had nothing to do with it! I'm not prejudiced!"

*D*o you think the government is doing a good job? No. It's not equal enough for poor people—money-wise, job-wise, school-wise, education-wise. In some ways, I think they're not being fair at all because they are making it hard for black people to live in nice areas and making stuff too expensive and the pay too low.

Education-wise, they're not giving everybody a fair opportunity to go to college. If you want to go to college, college is over $2,000. People have to pay over hundreds of dollars just to buy books. That's not fair because a lot of people don't have that money. The only way I think I can go to college is if I want to deal drugs again. I don't want a loan because you have to pay all that back and I don't see why you have to get a loan to get an education.

They are making it so now you can't get no kind of job unless you have a high school diploma—you can't even work at Burger King. It's too hard to even get a driver's license. People get really disgusted and get tired of dealing with it and they turn to something else, like dealing drugs or guns.

*H*ow does government affect your life? I don't know. I haven't dealt too much with the government.

*W*hat about the social services? Your social worker is probably a Maryland government employee. I guess they help you in different ways and stuff. They're okay, I guess. They tried to put me in a foster home, but I don't like foster homes. I don't like people trying to pretend to be my parents when they are not.

But they are doing a good job, in a way. Because like at one place I may go after Fellowship of Lights, St. Anne's Maternity Home, you stay there for a year, earn a G.E.D., learn a trade; plus your child goes to church. My child's first year, he or she will be brought up religiously and after that I could take it over.

*W*hat do you think of Bill Clinton? I hope he's better than Bush. Bush stuck his nose into other countries' business and started a lot of stuff that shouldn't have been started. Clinton is already starting to cut the budget stuff down. I think he'll be a good president. If I was old enough to vote, I would have most definitely voted for him.

*D*o you think teens care about the country? There are many times I've been in a room with fifteen drug dealers and we've all just started talking about what's going on in the news. There are times we'll sit down and we'll watch the news. You even see a lot of us reading newspapers and stuff.

I'm a teenager. I care a heck of a lot what goes on in our country. I hate wars. I believe in peace and stuff.

*W*hat is your idea of a good citizen? Oh, I don't know. Any type. I couldn't answer that one because anybody can be a good citizen. Even a drug dealer can be a good citizen, maybe not a law-abiding citizen, but a good citizen.

*I*f you could live in any country in the world, which one would you pick and why? South Africa. I would love to go over there and help abolish apartheid and free South Africans over there. I'd like to help them and be a white activist against the white supremacists.

I've been involved in little organizations with apartheid. I've helped make signs for a lot for them and there is even a few times that I was given flyers and sent into real bad, black-populated areas to pass them out. And they'd be like, "A white person doing this, trying to abolish apartheid? This is something new!" It wasn't in no big organizations; it was just something a lot of us could get together and do.

*W*hich one of your rights as an American do you value the most? Freedom of speech. Because I think it's important for people to speak their peace. If somebody has something they gotta say, then let them speak it. Don't try holding them like Nelson Mandela. He was locked up for it. If I have something I want to talk about, like apartheid, stuff like that, if I want to speak about it, I'll speak my peace. If people don't like it, they can arrest me; I don't care.

*W*hat do you think your responsibilities are as an American? Voting— if you're old enough to vote. Because it's important to let the U.S. decide who they want their president or congresswoman to be. If we don't vote, then we get some dippy like President Bush or Reagan to be our president.

*D*o you trust politicians? No. They say things just to get picked but they don't do it, so I don't trust them. I can't remember who it was, but somebody said they were going to lower taxes and help get jobs back, and then that never happened. Taxes got higher. There are a lot of politicians I don't trust.

*W*hat is your American dream? My dream, what I want to be and stuff like that? I would say my American dream is to help teenagers like myself get on the right track. I also want to get my G.E.D. and go to police school to be a narcotics officer—a narc. I want to be an undercover officer and bust people with drugs. A lot of adventure in it, I guess.

There are two narcotics officers in Baltimore County that I have become really close to. I consider them basically the only family I have. I really look up to them for what they did for me: they got me out of selling drugs. That's why I want to be a narcotics officer, because I want to be like them.

A lot of narcotics officers that I have worked with say half the stuff I would tell them, they didn't even know. I'd be good at it because I know a lot of the routines drug dealers go through.

*W*hat do you think America is going to be like in fifty years? I think that our country is on a downhill slide. I think after maybe two years with Clinton it might go back up the hill. After a few years, either there won't be the U.S., or hopefully our country will be better than what it has been.

Right now I think the most common deadly disease is AIDS. Hopefully in fifty years, AIDS will just be like another venereal disease that can be treated and cured.

*D*o you think there are a lot of other people like you out there? Oh, yeah. Lots. There are a lot of people—twelve- or thirteen-year-olds, too—dealing drugs, living off the streets, being prostitutes. I think it takes a lot of guts for a little white girl to deal drugs. It's so dangerous. So many young girls are prostitutes 'cause they are afraid. Many of them are homeless. I chose drug dealing over prostitution because I have respect for my body—I would never do that. The only way I had to survive was to sell drugs.

*W*hat would you tell people who want to help people like you? I would tell them to go for it and try. Get them legal jobs that pay enough, help them out with their own apartments and stuff, show them that it's not so bad doing it the legal way.

"It's supposed to be a land of opportunity."

Keith Lew Wong

Keith Wong tells of the time when his grandfather had to sneak into the United States from China because immigration laws prevented him from coming here. His grandfather was then detained for six months in a cold, lonely cell at Angel Island. Keith also knows that with dedication, persistence, and hard work, his family has firmly and successfully established itself in San Francisco, California, after three generations. Those experiences have influenced Keith in fundamental ways: he works diligently to be successful in school, treasures his parents, brother, and sister (and dog, Riki), and hopes to have an impact on the world—maybe even to be the person who discovers the cure for AIDS. Although his country didn't warmly welcome his ancestors, sixteen-year-old Keith loves the United States and feels he has the responsibility to help others and be informed about issues. Now, Keith, who can rarely keep a smile from his face, hopes to become an Eagle Scout and attend the college of his choice.

*H*ow did your family come to the United States? Before they came here, my grandparents lived in little villages in China full of people with the same last name. Like there would be a Lew village and Quan village, and they would marry between villages. Each house was a couple of stories tall, and there was a drainage ditch outside the house which sometimes flooded over. There was a latrine about a hundred yards away, so they all had to go to the bathroom there. They usually worked in rice fields outside the village. Everybody worked cooperatively.

They couldn't come over to the United States easily because there were a lot of restrictions on immigration back in the 1900s and 1920s, like the Chinese Exclusion Act. But in 1906, the Great Fire in the San Francisco earthquake destroyed most of the immigration records. And so the citizens here could claim that they had many sons and daughters back in China. People in China would take those family names to be allowed to immigrate; this was called a "paper name." It was the only way to get in. My mom's father came over to America in 1914 when he was eight years old by using a paper name. Their fake last name was Wong. After they came to America, they changed it back to their real name, Quan. On my Dad's side, his father also used Wong as a fake name. My real last name is my middle name—Lew.

After they got here, most Chinese immigrants had to go to Angel Island for detention. My grandfather went there for six months or so. Everybody was housed in little cells. Angel Island is famous for all the poems that were etched into the walls by people that were there. They wrote poems about their sorrows and stuff like that.

> **For what reason must I sit in jail? It is only because my country is weak and my family poor.**
>
> A poem from a cell on Angel Island

Many immigrants moved to Chinatown first, but now Chinatown is really crowded. It really stinks sometimes on certain streets because the homeless hang around there and the merchants are just dirty—they don't really clean up their own sidewalks and they fill them up with trash. There's a lot of tourists around, so it's pretty crowded with people shopping. And at night time it's not that safe to walk around Chinatown, because all the Asian gangs usually run around then and hang out in theaters or a park. Most Chinese people have moved into the Sunset District. They worked hard enough to afford a better place to live in than just an apartment in Chinatown.

I think [the immigration laws and detentions] were wrong, but I guess in those times, everybody was against immigration and against outsiders coming in, thinking that they would be changing and diversifying the American way of life. But it's supposed to be a land of opportunity. They should have let everybody in. I think it's good that they finally did because now everybody can share each other's points of view and customs. I think that America is pretty culturally diverse, well at least California and San Francisco.

hat kind of Chinese customs does your family follow? Well, there's the Moon Festival. We usually eat moon cake to signify that. Moon cake is kind of a Chinese version of fruit cake. I don't really like it. It's hard and sweet, with some kind of beans in it.

And then we have the Chinese New Year. My dad makes those red signs with little sayings like "good luck bringing in the New Year." My mom makes lanterns out of the money they give out during Chinese New Year. There's customary food that you eat, like moo shu pork and stuff called dzai—a vegetarian dish. We usually go to visit the family on New Year's. The Chinese New Year's parade is also a big thing—lots of tourists go there. I think I went to one or two before; my dad was in it one time. But I think once you see it, there's not much reason to go again because they just have the same line dances and a dragon and those big guys on stilts.

There's a lot of other holidays, but we don't really observe some of them. My parents aren't that traditional because we're a Christian family and we celebrate all the Christian holidays. We just celebrate the major Chinese holidays because it's good to keep in touch with your own ancestry and your own customs, and at the same time, have the American ones, like the Fourth of July.

Church is very big in my life right now. We go to church every Sunday. I think Christian values are what I live with every day—how

I deal with hardships and the suffering that goes on. I think Christianity has taught me how to get out there and give a lot. I do day camp in the summertime to help kids learn and try to be better people.

*T*ell me about the Chinese education that you've had. My parents encouraged me to go to Chinese school when I was in first grade. I went to Chinese schools in Chinatown, Saturdays from nine to twelve. I memorized old poems, stories, and learned new vocabulary words. We had a test every week too. I haven't been going though since I graduated from eighth grade.

The best thing that I learned was the old poems, because they usually told about how life was back in China, like farming or feudal wars a long time ago. There is one lesson I liked about this guy who tells a sort of ten commandments of life, saying how to respect your parents and respect everybody else around you. And he told about life and if there are bad times, what to do. Probably the hardest thing he said to do was respecting what your parents say all the time, because your views are a lot different than your parents' views. But I get along well with my parents.

I speak Chinese pretty well. I used to speak it better before, but over the years I haven't spoken it that much. I used to speak a lot of Chinese with my parents when I was little, and with grandparents every time I saw them because they don't know any English.

*W*hat is it like to attend a magnet school like Lowell? It's a pretty tough transitional time, because junior high was so much smaller and a lot easier. I was spoiled in that I didn't really have to work hard for As in junior high. Then when I got to Lowell, I had to work hard just to get Bs. I work three and a half, sometimes four hours a night on homework. My mom's also making me prep for the SAT.

Lowell's stereotype is as a nerd school. [*Laughter*] It's a college preparatory school. Lowell has a lot of courses that most other schools in San Francisco don't have, like advanced placement and honors classes. You can select your own classes and your own time schedule. The majority of teachers at Lowell are very old, and I think these older teachers are a lot harder than the younger teachers that are coming out now.

I was wondering what you thought of the stereotype of Asian students as extremely smart. I'm sure you've heard that. Yes! [*Laughing*] I think that stereotype is true because most of the Asians around me are really smart. And I think it's because our ancestors had to work harder in China for everything they had. They had to work in the field every day. I think the view back in China was that America was this great land that you can find success in if you try hard enough, so they all try harder—and a lot of them succeed.

But there are problems with that. My school has a majority of Chinese students. So they're setting up new rules to limit the number of Chinese people going. You've got to get perfect scores to get in. But I heard of some people that did get everything perfectly and still didn't get in—just because they're Chinese. They're lowering the standards for other races and making the standards a lot tougher for Asians mostly. I guess they want to racially mix it. I think they should just let whoever's qualified come in.

How do you think the country's doing with discrimination? I think in San Francisco, it's not as bad. But down south, it's worse because, well, everybody stereotypes the South as being racist. We took a trip to Arizona because my dad had business there, and we went to see the Grand Canyon. There were hardly any other minorities there, and we'd get stares from people. Once we were in this store and one of the clerks was standing there and I asked her for help, and she just walked away. I found that surprising. I had to walk all the way around and ask somebody else.

So you've never had problems with discrimination? No, not around San Francisco. Although there's lots of kids that make fun of you some-times because you're Chinese or because they're black or white or anything. I think that kids like that are kind of ignorant when they make fun of each other. It's probably everywhere else, too. In San Francisco, they can just call you names or something, but they're not going to do anything. Once in awhile, there's some isolated incidents—I guess you would call them hate crimes—where they mess up a Vietnamese business or write messages on the walls. The people I hang around with are mostly Asian, but like in Boy Scouts, there's three Chinese guys, a couple of blacks, and the rest white. We have no problems hanging around each other.

What kind of gang problems do you have around here? In Chinatown and the Sunset District, there's a lot of Chinese gangs. They're into drugs, and a couple of weeks ago they got busted for running a prostitution ring in Pacifica, which is like a fifteen-minute drive from here. And then there's lots of kids that form big bunches. There's this one gang known as Lamb Boys because they all hang around this ice cream shop called Lamb's. All they do is steal—they're all dropouts. Most of them are seventeen or eighteen. I don't know if they work or not, or where they get their money.

There's other gangs, too. There are Mexican gangs and black gangs. Basically it's just racially separated gangs; there's really no integrated gangs except for in San Francisco, where there's lots of Taggers. That's what you call people who do graffiti. Taggers have like a nickname and they write it on the wall and that's called their tag. It's not just a certain race that does this; whites, blacks, and Chinese could be in the same group at the same time.

No one has ever tried to get me to join a gang—and I wouldn't do that. But the thing is also mainly the neighborhood you live in. In my neighborhood, things are good right now, but if I lived in the Sunset District, maybe I would associate with more Chinese gang kids my age. I think that's how it happens nowadays; you're just around them and get to know them and start hanging around with them.

What's the difference between the Asians who are doing really well in school and business and the ones who are dropping out of school and getting into trouble? I think the main difference is the parents. Of the kids that work hard, maybe their parents really encourage them to do better. I know a lot of dropouts that still live at home and their parents don't really care what they do—maybe because their parents just came over from China and have two jobs or something and they're never at home. So they can't even offer their kid any guidance. The only people the kids could hang around with was gangs and other kids that had no support from anybody at home either. So they just roam around together causing trouble.

Basically, my mom guided me, my brother, and my sister along on what to do. I'm going to the same high school that my brother and sister went to. My mom wants me to go to college. She's instilled our attitudes and our values. She only worked until about one o'clock when I was younger, so she was always there for me [after school]. And my dad always came home around dinner time, so I could talk with him too.

How did you get started in Boy Scouts? I knew a couple kids in my neighborhood and so I joined with them and we started this Cub Scout pack. Then, I joined a Boy Scout troop. It's a very good troop because I think the fathers are really dedicated to helping and they always take us camping and bike riding. We have a big trip every other year. Two years ago the trip was a week of horseback riding up in the Sierra Nevadas, near Lake Tahoe. We each took care of a horse—my horse was named Leona. And we rode with them out to the different campsites and down to lakes. They taught you how to ride going up and down steep hills, and you had to trust the horse the whole time. Going around the lakes was fun. But the old trail is pretty scary, because even though the horse is pretty sure-footed, sometimes they slip and you go, "Oh!"

Then I've gone to Boy Scout camp, where I earned more merit badges. There is a whole variety of merit badges, like environment, emergency preparedness, basketry, shotgun, and citizenship in the community, nation, and the world—that's where you learn about local, state, national, and international governments. After I'm done with those, I just have to do a service project to be an Eagle Scout. I might do something with a homeless shelter or go to a park and ask them what I can do. I think it should be something that would set you apart.

There has been a lot of controversy about God in Boy Scouts because the Scout oath is "On my honor I will do my best to do my duty to God and my Country." Some people don't like saying it's under "God"; they might have different beliefs of God or something like that. If it's the group belief that you have to be reverent to your God, that's their belief. I think it's okay. If you don't want to be part of it, then form your own group. Same as the gay thing in Boy Scouts. You know how they're saying they won't admit gays, it's bad? That's one of the Boy Scout values. Their rules are not to admit any gays into Boy Scouts. So if they don't want to change it, I don't think people should make them do that.

The Boy Scouts of America was founded February 8, 1910. As of 1992, there were 4.15 million members. In addition to the Boy Scout motto "Be prepared," the organization stresses a moral code, outdoor activity, progressive training rewarded with merit badges, and daily good deeds. The highest honor is the Eagle Scout badge.

What do you think is the most valuable thing you've learned in Boy Scouts? I think I've learned to work with other people more than in any other experience I've had. We do day camp for Cub Scouts, so I've learned to work with younger kids, kids my age, and kids older than I. And we have a concession booth at Cal-Berkeley football games. So there you would learn how to cooperate with people outside your group too, like the management of the concessions company. And you gotta be polite too. People usually complain about the high prices, 'cause a drink is like $2.75. You have to constantly work together [as a team]: like when you go camping—people need to work together to get the firewood, set up, cook, and clean up. So I learned to work with other people and respect their views.

Where have you learned the things that you know about government? I think I learned a lot in school. In eighth grade we read a lot of the Constitution and learned about the three branches. And right now in

U.S. history, we just finished the '40s and '50s, and also segregation of the schools. We learned what kind of power the Supreme Court had and what was in their jurisdiction. Like the *Brown v. Board of Education* case—whether it was their right or Congress's to say segregation is bad.

In Boy Scouts, we learned citizenship in the nation. We learned about the system of government and the branches: what each does, stuff like that. And then we learned what a good citizen is.

How would you describe a good citizen? Hanging out your flag would be one of the things a citizen should do. I think during the holidays you have to show [patriotism]. I also think [reciting] the Pledge of Allegiance is a big thing. And believing in your country also. You know how some people are saying, "Oh, Americans are all so bad"? They should just do something about it instead of complaining. I think that's what they should do.

So do you think the government is doing a good job? You could say they're doing a fair job. But the economy is still bad, and Clinton has to make all the cuts that he's making now in order for it to be better. Like those Air Force bases around here closing. I heard on the news the other day that traditionally after each base is closed, after a little hard time, that area does better afterwards. I think they said they have 3,000 people who were fired, but next time new businesses come in, 12,000 people will be hired. So I think it will be tough times for a little bit, but it will be better afterward.

I also think people made too much of a fuss over who Clinton was appointing, like that Zöe Baird. And they'd make a big deal if he hired his black Cabinet member or something. If he was qualified, then hire him. It didn't really matter. Everybody has to put the color of his skin to the side and just look at the qualifications, but I guess that's too hard to do because [skin color is] right there; it's so obvious.

What did you think of the presidential elections? I think it was dragged out a little bit too much. They gave the candidates so much time just to repeat themselves. Bush would just keep on going at the fact that Clinton avoided the draft and all that, and then Clinton would just say, "Oh, the economy's so bad." I also think Bush would have had a better chance if he had picked somebody else besides Quayle. Quayle isn't that bad; it's just things that he did were so stupid— like the potato thing—that everybody labeled him as not a good vice president.

Bush wasn't doing a good job at all as president. And I think we needed a new way of thinking instead of the Republican way, because we had Republicans for the past twelve years. I think I would have voted for Perot . . . well, realistically, I think Clinton. Perot's charismatic, he catches the crowd when he talks, very confident of himself, but the economy is basically all he preached. He didn't talk much about social plans and international things. So I don't know how good of a job he would have done. Also his vice president candidate, Admiral Stockdale, didn't know anything.

*W*hat do you think is the biggest problem facing the country? Most people would say the economy, but I think the only way you could have a good economy is to have jobs for everybody. So I think jobs are the most pressing thing in the nation right now. Like in the summertime when I look for jobs, I find that nobody's really hiring younger kids, because lots of adults don't have jobs.

And all the homeless people, they need to find jobs for them. We just learned about Roosevelt, how he had the WPA, CCC, and how he made the people work for what they wanted. Now, the people on welfare expect the government to give a lot. So I think Clinton has to find a way to find more jobs and distribute the jobs to the less fortunate.

I don't really know much about the welfare system. But from what my experience is, the welfare system is pretty easy to cheat. For example, the government subsidizes cheap housing projects for the Chinese people in Chinatown. I know a couple of people who live there, but they're living very well. Their parents are on welfare but yet can afford to buy a new car. Then, the government built new low-cost housing, and each person that lived in the projects had first dibs on it. So they just moved into a new house that's nicer than most houses out there that middle class people are working hard to have. So I think that's one way that the system maybe caters a little bit too much to them. The government gives too much and doesn't expect that much in return.

Do you think teenagers care about the country and are informed about issues? At Lowell, everybody knows a lot about the subjects right now in the world, but in the other schools, I find that people don't really care because their schools don't focus on the subjects and current events right now. I think that a majority of the kids probably don't really care about what's happening now, but as you get older, I guess it becomes more apparent to you.

Do you think Americans care about their country? No. I think they care most about themselves and they just expect to receive everything all the time. They expect the government to do everything for them, when they don't do anything for themselves to help their situation.

Do you think politicians are trustworthy? I think we expect them to be, but then there are a lot of politicians that are concerned only with themselves. I don't think they're really doing that much for the community or the citizens. They should stop arguing and try to reach a compromise.

And then there are just a lot of negative attitudes about the government, with all these groups like ACT-UP or those hippie-type groups, the pro-choice people, and all rap songs, too.

There is this rapper that went to Lowell. His stage name was Paris, and one of his songs is called "Bush Killer." That's obviously slanted towards President Bush. I think it makes a lot of people mad at Bush because Paris says something like, "Hey, look at the economy and stuff like that, it's pretty bad." And before the song starts, he plots out an assassination of Bush: like he's at the White House and he shoots him. So I think that shapes a lot of people's views, indirectly.

Do you think you would ever run for political office yourself? Well, I was a class officer for a couple years. It was basically a popularity contest. People aren't really concerned with your qualifications and what you can do. The other officers were just a group of popular kids who weren't really in touch with the other people.

That's why I don't think I would run. Well, if times got really bad and I really wanted to change things, then maybe I would try to get into politics. But I'm not that good of a public speaker.

What do you think is your most important right as an American citizen? I think that would be to an education at least through high school. Not everyone can afford college, but I think education up to high school is really important, because you can't really go anywhere without a high school diploma. At least they teach you the basic skills of what you need to succeed in the world.

If you had the opportunity to live anywhere in the world, including the United States, where would you choose? I like San Francisco the most, just because it's so culturally diverse. It's a beautiful city, I think. We take everything for granted, but we have everything we ever need here— we can plant our own food and all that, too.

I also think America is still the best country in the world. There's a lot of problems in America, but not as bad as the other countries. Like there's no wars being fought; there's no terrorism within America, except I guess you could call the Waco, Texas, thing or the bomb in New York a form of it. But like in England, they have the IRA and stuff like that.

*W*ho are your heroes? My heroes? I don't think I like one person for everything they are. I think that everybody has like sports heroes or something. They might be good in sports, but maybe their personal life may not be that good. Like Michael Jordan, he's one of the best basketball players, but he owed a lot of money to bettors. Other people might think of him as a hero, but I don't. Just because he's a good basketball player and he can say he's sorry for it, people say, "Oh, okay, let's forgive him." But I think people should stick to people close to home and look at what they've done to help other people. I think people that volunteer at these homeless shelters are the people that give so much and make a difference in the world.

*I*n what way would you like to make a difference? Maybe if I worked for the Environmental Protection Agency or DEA—if I could go out there and bust some of the bad guys or bring in somebody that was real bad. Or if I go into chemistry or something, maybe I could discover a cure for AIDS! Well, maybe not that big, but anything that would make a little bit of a difference in the world would be good.

*H*ow would you describe yourself? I'm just an average kid with pretty high expectations, though I'm not sure if I'll reach all of my expectations! I'm going to try. I think I care a lot about other people too, like the homeless. I think I have some sort of intelligence. I have some basic skills. That's how I describe myself, just your everyday person.

*H*ave you heard the term "American dream"? What's yours? I think back a long time ago the American dream was when you came over to America and made a name for yourself and did better than you would have before. I think right now the American dream is just getting your education and finding a job, and not living in poverty and supporting yourself and your family. And just living happily. I think that's the American dream right now.

I just want a good job that I can support my family with. Work with people that are easy to work with. Belong to organizations like Boy Scouts and help the younger kids shape their views so that they can grow up to be successful, too. That's what I want to do, to help other people.

What do you think the country's going to be like in fifty years? I hope that America would be the model for all the nations in the world and that maybe all the other nations would be like America in fifty years. Maybe everybody would have a democracy and everybody would have an equal say and there wouldn't be any racism. I think racism by then will probably be gone, because everybody grows out of everything. I don't think there will be any more wars.

I hope that America has a good president that everybody likes and that there wouldn't be any different views between Republicans and Democrats and others. I wish the parties would all work together. I hope that in fifty years everybody will work for the common good. I think it's possible, if everybody tries hard enough to work with each other and just tries to meet halfway. That's what I want America to be in fifty years.

"We need a chance."

Damion W.

Damion W. felt that as a youth in depressed South Central Los Angeles, there were few job options besides fast food. He wanted clothes, freedom, and a place where someone would always be there. He couldn't get much help from his divorced parents—a hard-working, single mother and a traveling father—but he found easy money in drug dealing and moral support in the Raymond Street Crips. The gang became his family, but at a price. Before it was over, gang-related violence claimed the lives of friends and family, and almost Damion himself. But he now has hope. Sent to a juvenile detention camp for bank robbery, he swears that the experience changed his life. At eighteen, Damion doesn't trust others and keeps his guard up at all times; showing emotion is definitely off-limits. Although the emotional and physical scars of his gang life are finally healing, Damion still faces many challenges, including the task of keeping his daughter out of the cycle of loneliness, disenchantment, and violence that haunts low-income, urban communities and turns teens to gangs.

***W**hy did you get involved with gangs?* Well, my mother and father got divorced when I was eight years old. It was just a single parent, me, and my three brothers. My father was an insurance agent, so that meant he had to be out in the field all the time. It wasn't that my parents were struggling with money, but there was certain things that I wanted for myself like clothes, jewelry, shoes, stuff like that, that I knew my dad wasn't able to get for me. There was nobody there to watch us, and I had nothing to do. My brother used to sell dope, and I caught an interest in making money like that. I started calling people around and say, "Man, I want to start selling dope."

When I was selling, I would just walk around, and people would be asking, "What you got or what you need?" I was worried because I know I was doing something that was illegal, and where I used to sell dope was right around the corner from the sheriff's station. But I made $300 a day selling drugs.

Then I got hooked up with the Raymond Street Crips when I was twelve years old. I had to get jumped in. That means you had to fight somebody. I was in a small, compact room, and there was about fifteen people, and they were like, "Pick somebody you want to fight with." We just had to win a fight, that's it. I was in. We usually hung out on 120th and sold dope in that alley right there.

***W**hy is there such rivalry between the Crips and the Bloods?* It started way, *way* back—over a jacket. It was like somehow or another everybody used to get along, but then they didn't want to negotiate with one another anymore. They started killing each other once in a while. It's all it was. The Crips' color is any color blue; the Bloods' color is red.

I never got in any kind of fight with any other Bloods, but it was other Crips gangs I had fights with. Somehow Crips fight with other Crips over minor things. But when it comes down to the Bloods, it's like, well, you see a Blood and you want to kill them if you're a Crip. That's the same thing with them. They see you and they gonna try to kill you. That's all it was.

So what did you like about being in the Crips? It ain't really nothing good about gangs in my eyes right now. You just get locked up. But back then it was like . . . you know where you can go, you know where you can hang out at. If you had any problems at home, you talk to your homeboys. If you don't have no money, somebody will have some money to give you. It was like I was in my own little world, you know. I have friends go to jail every day. And it was like it wasn't no big thing; it was crazy-like. It was all there was to me—I had nothing else to fall up on. It's like a big family.

There's a lot of drive-by shootings; there's a lot of gangbangers that just don't care what they do. You know they say if you ain't gonna die one day, they're gonna die soon. There's two types of gangbangers to me. There's good gangbangers and bad gangbangers. There's gangbangers that's all about drive-bys, stealing, and killing; there's gangbangers that are all about money. [The ones about money are] good because there ain't nobody going to hire them. It'll be hard for

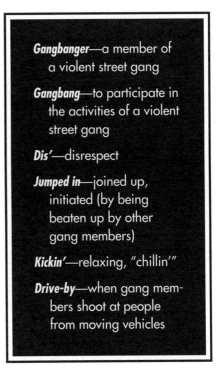

Gangbanger—a member of a violent street gang

Gangbang—to participate in the activities of a violent street gang

Dis'—disrespect

Jumped in—joined up, initiated (by being beaten up by other gang members)

Kickin'—relaxing, "chillin'"

Drive-by—when gang members shoot at people from moving vehicles

them to get hired without no high school diploma. Even a college degree or something. Right now that's their only choice.

I worked at Burger King, Taco Bell, Wendy's. It was all right. There was one particular job I had that I had to quit because it was in a Blood neighborhood. Some of the Bloods that was in that neighborhood knew me and they used to come up there every day just looking for me. They's looking like, "Where that crab at?"—you know that's how they dis' Crips—"I know there's a crab, where he at?" So I had to quit. I didn't want to bring my problems off on all the people there.

*H*ave you ever been really scared? Yes. Once I went to go put gas in my brother's car, and about seven Bloods hopped out of a truck and came towards the car I was in. They probably didn't know who I was, but they knew that car. They started busting on it and shooting at me. When it was over, the car just had a lot of bullet holes, that was it. They didn't hit me.

And when I was in the drive-by shooting, that was my scariest, *scariest*. I was just hanging in the alley and a car came through. I recognized it and said, "Man, watch out for this car!" And I just started running, but before I could run and jump the fence, I got shot right down here [*pointing to lower back*]. I don't know the person, but I know what gang it was.

I told my homeboys not to call an ambulance. I was scared of going to the hospital, period. If you're going to die, you don't have to go in the hospital. You can die right there. My mother's a nurse and she took the bullet out 'cause it wasn't all the way in. It took about a week or two to heal. I was all right after that.

My homeboys said they was going to retaliate for me, but I said like, "Don't even worry about it, I'm still living." But they got their own mind; they'll do what they want to do.

That whole experience just got me more involved in gangs. Around then, one uncle and two cousins of mine got killed over gang activity. I was going crazy. We would just walk down the street and take people's money. I moved away from my home and I was staying with my homeboy. Just going crazy.

*W*hat changed you? When I got locked up for bank robbery and I had to do a year and a half away from my mother and father and my brothers. I really don't know why I did it. A friend had called me, and he just told me about this bank we could rob. And we did. I got caught later on that night. They got me on the videotape.

My mother was shocked when she read my file. Before that, she didn't know I was a gangbanger. I didn't show her the gangbanger side of me 'cause I know that she would've been hurt. All that time, my father had an idea that I was a gangbanger but he never said anything 'cause he had no proof.

I went to juvenile hall, and I wasn't trying to fight the case—I had admitted to the crime. But they kept on telling me I had to wait to go back to court. That process took like three months. Then they sentenced me to a juvenile detention camp called Camp Kilpatrick.

Camp was very interesting. I played football and that's another thing I do now way different from the gang life. At camp there was Bloods on the team, but it wasn't like we ever really got into it 'cause we all knew what we had to do—win our football games the best way we could. And the coaches were always right there if you needed them.

I got out of Camp Kilpatrick this January. I'll be on probation for about a year. I have to meet with my probation officer once a week. It's good 'cause I have someone to talk to if I have any problems with my child or anything. He wants to listen.

I think it's the best thing for me 'cause I know if I wouldn't have got arrested that day, I'd probably got killed the next day. There's a reason for everything. I don't smoke weed no more, I don't drink no more, and I don't hang around with the people I used to hang around with. I learned my lesson. I feel I can make it on my own; I don't need no gang to help. That's what really changed my life.

Do your gang friends accept that? Just the ones that are older, like nineteen, twenty years old. They understand where I'm coming from. The young ones know how I was, and they like, "How can he change?" But everything's possible. Some of them say, "Well, I ain't gonna mess with it no more either; I better chill." But I never know.

What do you think would help other people like you that maybe don't get arrested, that don't get that chance? They need to talk to somebody. That's all. Nowadays, they ain't going to let just anybody walk in our neighborhood. The best way they can get help is to help themself.

What people have to realize is that gangbangers aren't bad people. They ain't criminals. Some of them, they be gangbangin' to help their families, or just to get by. It's a place to go. It's a way to make it.

We need something respectable to do, a way to earn money without selling drugs. We need a chance.

*D*o you see any ways that the national government affects your life? I don't really know.

*I*f you could change one thing, what would it be? The gang situation. Just give them a different outlook on life. Maybe if some of the gang-bangers around here went through what I went through—being locked up—they'd probably have a different outlook on life. That's what I feel.

I'd get them jobs. Just a nice, decent job they can fall up on. They need a check coming in. I have homeboys right to this day that tell me, "Man, if I had a job, I'd stop everything."

*W*hat is it like to have a child at your age? She's nice. She cries, but she don't cry too much. She's a nice little girl. It feels good to be a dad in a way, but it's a lot of responsibility to have a child. There's diapers, running to the hospital, and food. I can barely keep clothes on my back, and have to keep clothes on hers. I don't live with her, though. I stay with my mother.

*H*ow are you going to keep your little girl from getting involved in a gang? I won't let her listen to certain rap music. There's a lot of rap music that's too bad for little kids. Some of it's okay. The majority of the rap music I listened to are the songs by Crips. Ice Cube, he used to be a Crip. I knew him; I used to go to high school with him. I saw him about three weeks ago. He came over where he used to hang out at and got a couple people and had them start rapping. They're called the Lynch Mob.

*W*hat you think of the controversy about Ice-T's song "Cop Killer"? Well, it's like, the way cops be killing people nowadays, you know. [*Shrugs*] I lost two close homeboys of mine—they got killed by police. So I don't really care too much about police. I don't know exactly how my friends got killed. All I know is I was on my way over to their house, and my homeboys said police was in the alley chasing them. About twenty minutes later, the only thing I heard was gun shots. And around the corner we found them dead.

> " *I have 50 cases. I would estimate that about 75 percent of my cases will reoffend. Of my current cases, Damion has shown the most promise. He has the potential to do well in school and is an excellent athlete.* "
>
> Steve Wells, D.P.O., Metro Gang Unit, South Central Probation Office

*W*hat do you think about discrimination? Do you think that things are getting better? I don't know if they're getting better or worse. I guess I was treated differently for being a gangbanger. When I used to go to football squad meetings, you know, even then the police always used to just follow us around like we were troublemakers. But sometimes gangbangers do have the will to help their self, you know. And everybody thinks we're all just troublemakers.

*D*o you think there's any reason for treating gang members differently? No.

*W*hat do you think about the riots around the Rodney King trial? I think the riot will go out [happen again] not just because of the situation with Rodney King, but because of the guys who got arrested for pulling that man off his truck. If the homeboys get sentences, there is gonna be another riot. I can't say why or how. You know, some of these people, they getting tired of it—getting abused by the police. They just want to retaliate. They don't need no big excuse.

If you could live anywhere in the world including the United States, where would you live? Right here. I was raised right here. I probably don't like the social environment, but it's me, it's what I want to do, it's where I want to stay.

Of all your rights as an American citizen, which one do you value the most? I don't know.

Well, what rights do you think you have? There are a lot of rights. I don't know which ones I have, but I know I got rights.

Like what? Think about maybe what you've heard about other countries. I don't know nothing about other countries.

What about the court system. Did you have rights when you went to court? I had the right to remain silent. The whole thing, I don't know how you say it, but the whole thing.

The right to speak, I guess that's what I would say I would never give up. The right to do what I want to do.

In the United States, you have certain rights like freedom of speech. Do you think that you have responsibilities too? No. [*Shaking head*] No, I don't owe anything. But whenever there's a point where I am able to help, I know I can go back down to the neighborhood and help. Kind of put money in or pay somebody to get the graffiti off the walls. Because that's where I came from. You just can't leave behind something like that—well, I know I can't.

How would you describe yourself? I'm an intelligent young man who might do something with his self. I keep everything organized. I like decency. I keep myself clean. I am trying to improve my reading skills by reading more and more.

*D*o you think teenagers are interested in what's going on in the country? A lot of teenagers nowadays don't know nothing. They just go to school so they can buy clothes or whatever. Some students don't get involved in class and just be sitting there doing nothing.

*W*hat do you think politicians do? People like mayors and senators and the president? I don't know what they be doing.

*D*o you think politicians are trustworthy? Would I trust them? No. [*Shaking head*] If they was doing the right thing, there wouldn't be so much crime in Los Angeles. If they cared what I thought, they'd lower taxes. They ain't going to help me. You gotta help yourself. I'm going to do my own thing. It's just part of life.

*W*ould you ever run for office yourself? No. [*Firmly*] I just can't see myself running for nothing. It's not that I think I can't do it. I just won't run for it. Not my type of business. I am better at mechanic stuff, stuff I can do with my hands. Construction work, stuff like that. Not being cramped up in an office all day. In the long run, I want to go into the insurance business with my father.

*A*re you going to vote in the next election? Un-uh. They don't need my vote. If they win, they win; if they don't, they don't. I would vote for "none of the above." I don't know. I don't know about them people. It matters; it's just not something I want to do.

***W**ho are your heroes?* My mom. She's my hero, my best friend. Just by being the person she is. She's always there for me no matter what, no matter what I do. She came and saw me every week at Camp Kilpatrick. I only saw my father at my football games. My mom was there every fourth day. I would like to be like her—patient like her, polite like her, a lot of stuff.

***W**hat is your idea of a good citizen?* Me! [*Smiles*] I'm a good citizen now, doing what I am supposed to do—not doing nothing illegal. I live a nice, quiet life. That's the way I like it.

***W**hat do you think the country will be like in fifty years?* In different parts of the country, things are getting worse. Like cities, like L.A. Everyday, somebody is gettin' killed. I don't really see nothing new happening. But hopefully Bill Clinton will get around to it. So far, I think our man, Bill Clinton, will be all right. He wants to help us start getting jobs. That would really change things.

***W**hat do you think you will be able to accomplish in your life?* I have a lot of confidence in myself now. I know I can do anything I set my mind to. What might slow me down, though, is my family. If my child is sick, I have to take care of her; that's my duty. I won't always be able to do what I want anymore.

***A**re there things that you could do that might help the country to be a better place?* No. [*Pause*] Well, if I could become a professional football star, I think it would change a lot of people's lives. To see me, an ex-gangbanger on TV, playing football. Like if they say, "He can do it, I know I can do it, too." I'd go back to the old neighborhood and go to the local schools and talk to them about joining gangs and the gang life. Tell them I been through all of it, and it ain't worth it.

In the *Country*

"It's what you make of it."

Elizabeth Sibrian

Who do you suppose picked those tender, plump blueberries that are in the supermarket at the height of summer? How do Christmas trees always have that perfect, triangular shape come December? The berry hand-picking and the tree shearing could very well have been done by eighteen-year-old Elizabeth Sibrian, one of her younger brothers or sisters, her parents, or her grandparents, as the entire family migrates every year to work on harvesting crops. The days in the fields last from sunrise to sunset, and the work often results in sore backs and bleeding fingers, but it doesn't get Elizabeth down. Lively and energetic, she's determined to make the best of her experiences and herself—she wants to be the first in her family to attend college and become a working professional. When they're not on the road, the Sibrian family lives in Mission, Texas, a small town on the Mexican border. Though Elizabeth feels strong ties to Mexican culture, she loves the United States, where she believes life offers unfettered opportunities and hope for a better future.

ell me about migrant work. What is a year like? We leave early in the spring. So I have to get all my grades and schoolwork finished early.

My dad locks up the house. He puts boards on the windows, 'cause if people know you're not home they will take something. The trip is long and hard. I always ride in the front because I'm the one who reads the maps, and so I tell my dad, "Well, let's take this east; or we go west here" or whatever. It's a lot of fun. I'm also the one who tries to keep my dad from falling asleep.

We stop along the way at gas stations or at McDonald's. Most of the time, we don't eat inside; we just eat in the parking lot. There is a lot of people staring at us. 'Cause there is a bunch of colored people— like us, we're brown—and most of the people from those states are white, so if they see a whole bunch of us they turn and they stare. Sometimes they ask questions.

Most of the people are nice. I like to talk to the different people. We never got into trouble—well, just once—but it wasn't really trouble. This man came up to us and he says, "You guys Mexicans?" And we said, "Yeah, we're going to go up north working." So he starts talking to us and started telling us that in that town—it is somewhere in Indiana—they don't like blacks, and they don't like Mexicans, or whatever. So he tells us, "Well, you probably want to leave as soon as possible." It's hard to intimidate us. But he was doing it for our own good basically; I don't know, maybe some towns are like that.

We spend two or three months a year in Michigan. When I was fourteen, it was my grandparents, my uncle and my aunt, my father, my two brothers, and me. My youngest brother was ten years old when he started—he couldn't work, but came for the company. I had to be without my mom for all that time, and my mom and I were really close. My dad wouldn't let me talk on the phone with her because every time I talk I start crying, and then my mom would start crying. Then he would worry that my mom would be crying and she might get sick or whatever. So I would write her long letters. But always the hardest thing was being away from my mom.

We did that for like three years, and then my dad finally said that he couldn't handle it, being without my mom. So my mom quit her job as a seamstress, and now it's more fun, because we have my mom and my sister now. The whole family was there—nineteen people in this huge house. So we're never lonely.

I don't think migrant work is hard because you're with the people you love, and it's not like you get a beast or anything [for a boss]. The farmers are very nice—because we're providing a service and they're helping us by giving us a job. So we really have to respect them. We all get along and everything is fine.

One controversy about migrant work is that some farmers expose their workers to dangerous pesticides. Have you had any experiences with that?

We never had problems. They do use them, but not harsh pesticides. Like the first farm we did. These blueberries had like this orange—I don't know what it was—not bacteria, but like moss on them. So he would spray them one day, and then we wouldn't pick that field like for two or three days.

> Any child who has moved with his or her parents for the purpose of agriculture or fishing within the previous twelve months is classified as a current migrant by the Department of Education.

We've never encountered problems like that 'cause they have to abide by the laws, and they get checked a lot. That the housing facilities—everything—is in check, and that we're not being abused or cheated or anything. We get food stamps, and they pay for our housing and our utilities.

It's not hard work. I mean, I enjoy being in the field all day and since you don't talk to anybody, I get to think. I have a big imagination, so I keep busy on one subject the whole day. Migrant work, it's what you make of it. I don't think it's terrible. Migrant work taught me the value of the dollar and a lot of responsibility. I understand how hard it is now to want something so bad and not be able to buy it. But I really like migrant work. It's a new place and new people. And I think it is a great experience.

*D*o you earn enough money in the summer to live on all year round? Usually it's just for payments. Like this last summer we worked to pay our rent, you know, to advance several months of rent. Now we ran out of money, so we're depending on the food stamps to eat. My mom applied for assistance because there are no jobs around here—it's really hard if you don't have a degree of some kind. Because I am considered an adult I don't get any money, but my sister and my little brother do. We get a few dollars a month, and it helps a lot with the payments and the bills.

We have to depend a lot on government help. Because I've seen what it does, you know, having to depend on the government for aid, I want so bad to go to college and get an education. Then I can support my family, and I can get my mom and dad off the fields because they've been doing it all their lives. That is why working hard is so important.

See this is what it is—the migrant cycle. If your parents do it, it's likely that a lot of the kids are going to do it, and then they end up getting married to someone who is a migrant. So then the cycle continues. There are some who do get a permanent job or they go to college and then the cycle stops.

It's likely that my generation—we're going to keep doing it for a long time, and I don't want to do that. It's great, but it's not something that I want to do my whole life, you know. Especially if I have kids, I don't want them to go through what I've been going through.

*H*ow is U.S. education different from that in Mexico? In Mexico, it's only free up to the sixth grade, so if you want to keep on going, you pay. Usually the schools are miles away from all the little towns. All the girls end up getting married real young, and the boys go work in the fields or whatever they can find. There are some who have the money to pay and keep on going and be teachers or lawyers or whatever. So there is a lot of difference. Here, it's free through high school, unless you go to a private school. And the books are free and free lunch. Lunch is really important—no food, then no energy, so you really can't do anything.

Here, anybody can go to college if they really wanted to. In Mexico, not everyone can go, so there is always a restriction because of money.

It's not as easy for them as it is for us to go to college. Even if I have to end up paying for most of it, I think I would do it. But the federal aid, the money that is free, is the best.

Migrants do get a lot of benefits, more benefits than regular students. We have counselors specified for us. We have programs specified for us like the CAMP* scholarship. I've talked to a lot of my friends who want to go to college. Their parents are teachers or whatever and they make good money, but they don't have that money to put towards college. They are classified as good income families, so they don't qualify for any scholarships. They tell me that it's good being poor, because you get so much help and everything, and I'm really thankful that I'm going to get so much. Because if it wasn't for all the help I'm going to get, I don't know if I would be able to pay for college. The loans get expensive.

If you could live anywhere in the world, where would you live? I really love it here. Poor here is considered rich in Mexico. But I love Mexico a lot. I love being Mexican. Our culture is just something. We have great culture and a lot of pride. Us Mexicanos, we are great people. [*Laughing*] My favorite customs are tamales at Christmas, the Three Kings day, the little things, the piñatas. The way we celebrate family is so fantastic. Like the Quinceñera. That's when a young Mexican woman turns fifteen, we are into womanhood. It's like sweet sixteen but a sweet sixteen party is nothing like a Quinceñera. I didn't get one because we couldn't afford it. But basically, what we do, the daughter is escorted by her parents to the church, and there is a mass. We wear beautiful long dresses, usually pink. We have fourteen maids who supposedly represent each year of your life. And we have a huge party; everybody is invited, not just family members, everybody. The whole family is celebrating you, your birth, and you turning into a woman. It's great.

But I like living in the United States. I am glad that I have both worlds. I don't think I could live in any other country. I value being an American—it's a good place to be.

The College Assistance Migrant Program (CAMP) provides migrant students with tutoring, counseling, and financial aid for their first year of college.

*W*hat do you think are your rights as an American? Free speech.
Everything in the Bill of Rights. I have all those amendments; I have
all those rights—freedom of speech, religion, everything. I can say
whatever I want, because I am allowed to. Right to bear arms. I can
do mostly everything that is in the law, but not beyond the law.
'Cause nobody, not even the president, is allowed outside of the law.

I value free speech the most. Because I like to talk a lot, and in some
countries you can't say whatever you want. I know that I have a lot
to say, and sometimes it might not be positive or people might be
offended or think differently, but I can't be arrested or put in jail.

The most important right is being free. I have seen what [not being
free] does to other countries, like in the Soviet Union, all those
years—how harsh! I felt for the young people, that if they didn't want
to be a certain person, the government required them to do it. And
gosh, here I am, I can be anything I want—if I want to be a politician,
or if I want to be a nurse, whatever. I can do that because the government in this country allows me to, gives me that right. I like to
make my own decisions.

*W*hat do you consider your responsibilities as an American citizen? Voting.
Obeying the law. Respect for property. If it doesn't belong to me,
don't destroy it. Respect everybody. Stop the killing. The main one
is voting, and just having pride in your country, and being thankful
for all of the benefits we get.

I voted [in the primary elections]! That was the highlight of my eigh-
teenth birthday. And I'm going to vote [in the presidential election]. I
can't wait. I really have a say-so in the government! If I voted for
them and they are not doing what should be right, then I have a right
to complain. I finally feel like I am part of something. And I finally
get to make a difference because every vote does make a difference.

My mom took me to vote the last time. We walked from our house
all the way downtown, to the fire station. And then I registered and
they got my name down. That little curtain, I thought that was so
cute, getting in that thing. I was there for a long time. I wanted to
make the right decision, and I knew most of the candidates from the
interviews or whatever. And now, the president—wow—this is the

big one! This is the one I've been waiting for. If I was in bed with the worst sickness, I would still get up there and vote. Because it's going to affect your life for the next four years.

*D*o you think that you are obligated in any way to the community? You are not obligated. You're free. But I do feel obligated in a certain way. That is the reason I want to come back to the [Rio Grande] Valley. I want to leave the Valley and better myself, but I want to come back here to give back what I took out. I'm getting all these benefits. I am living a great life. A lot of people wouldn't consider it a great life, but I am happy the way I am. And I want to be able to spread this happiness onto everybody else.

You know what would be so neat doing, when I'm rich and famous? [*Laughing*] When I have the means, I would like to start my own scholarship fund. Because I know that I am relying on scholarships and grants to be able to study. Maybe just like $1,000 or $2,000. Anything helps, even $300 or $400. It would be for my grandkids, Mexican-American kids, maybe that want to go into the health field. Yeah, I am going to be biased. [*Smiling*]

*Y*our age group gets criticized for not caring, not being involved, not having a clue as to what's going on. Do you think that's fair? No. The older people are not giving us a chance to really speak out and say what we know. We are in the critical years. We are learning. We are being shaped to what we are going to become fifteen or twenty years from now. If they listen, they will learn something. They should give us a chance to make them proud of us. I know my parents are real proud of me. I am opening their doors along with mine. They ought to give us a chance to speak out and give them our view of the issues.

*W*hat do you think of Congress? Instead of working for us, they are working for themselves. The majorities run the whole show. Instead of being for the people, they benefit themselves. That is really terrible. They get their own selves in power, and they feel that they are the boss. It's for the power and prestige. They wrote all those checks and then denied writing them. They get free trips and it's on us. I count myself because I pay taxes. They should be thinking about the American people.

They do some good. I'm not going to deny it. Because if it wasn't for the government, I would not be getting all of these benefits. But I do know that there is a lot more that they can do for us.

***D*o you think minorities such as the Ku Klux Klan have the right to be heard?** They have a right because it is in the Constitution. But the hate is totally out of control. And I guess we are lucky that they are a minority because if it was majority, can you imagine where we would be?

I can't blame them for our problems. It's not their fault; it's everybody's fault. I am not just saying this because I am considered a minority in the world, but I am speaking as a human being. If I was anybody else, I would still feel like this, I think.

The reason there is so much racism is because of economic problems. It's depressing, like the violence in Los Angeles. It's terrible when people blame another color for their problems. Racism is just terrible. It really hurts. It not only affects the person you're racist against, it affects everybody in the whole world. Prejudice just doesn't make sense.

[We need to] educate all those that what they are doing is wrong. More love. This country needs a lot of love. We can turn it around. We are all brothers and sisters, one people. No matter what color you are. People find color as an excuse. All they see is problems being "caused by blacks, the whites, or Asians, or whatever." They are just finding a scapegoat. They don't realize that people are turned colors or their eyes are a certain way and their skin is a certain way because of the places that we were born in. Blacks were black because of the places they lived in. They needed that color and that body structure in order to survive in the environment that God put them into. And like us—the "short Mexicans"—we are like this because of the environment that God put us into.

I learned about this on TV. Tom Brokaw had a show on that. I watched the whole thing. He wanted to educate the children,

because they do what their parents and older brothers do. And I really took it to heart. There is no need for hate. Not in any society.

*H*ow did you learn about government and politics? Actually, I started mostly this year. That [government] class, I absorb every single thing our teacher says because it's real interesting. Before, all the information I had was from things I heard on the street and things I heard on TV. I am learning that it is not always the truth. There is a lot behind being the president. It's not something that because you are rich, you can get up there.

I think the TV is a powerful weapon, and if they really tell us what is going on, it would really help us. A lot of the stations are biased though. Like Channel One, I think they back up the Democrats a lot. And it should be both ways, Republicans and Democrats and Ross Perot. And they make fun because Quayle can't spell potato, but how many people can? Not a lot. Even the most educated college people don't know how to do certain things. I think they should concentrate more on the real issues than on the mudslinging.

*D*o you think the media are the ones that concentrate on the mudslinging or is it the candidates? Them too. They want it, to see the other one down. The real funny one years ago was when the vice president candidates, Lloyd Bentsen and Dan Quayle, were debating. Quayle said something about that everybody saw him as resembling John Kennedy, and then Mr. Bentsen says, "Well, I knew Mr. Kennedy and you are no John Kennedy." That was below the belt. Good comeback, but come on, concentrate on the real issues!

They are mature men, they want to be the number one guy of this whole nation and the world, and they are acting like little kids. That's what you expect from someone who is running for president of the school, saying we are going to have parties every Friday and this and that. But not from forty-, fifty- or sixty-year-old men running the country. They should concentrate on the real issues.

*D*o **you trust politicians?** Are you kidding? Not all of them. A lot of them can be trusted, a lot of them are trusted, but you can't trust every single one of them. No, it's not possible. It's just like you can't trust every teacher in school. There are a lot of corrupt politicians. The way a person can be trusted is if he doesn't do anything really, really wrong. We are all allowed to make mistakes once in awhile, but if those mistakes are going to start turning into excuses, there is no way you can trust them.

We do have a lot of power over who gets into office and who doesn't. We'll look for someone else the next time. And you can complain, you can write them, hope for the better, pray that they get struck by lightning! [*Laughing*] Well, no. Hope that they will realize that what they are doing is hurting many people.

*D*o **you think you could hold public office?** I need more input, more experience, and I need to grow and mature. It could be a possibility. It'll be cool because there are not many Hispanic or Mexican Americans in office. Can you imagine if I get up there? Or if I were vice president? I'd be happy being vice president. I could probably get up to be a representative or a senator, but there is so much to make a president. Look at all things you are going to do. Like me, if I don't have the military experience or all this political experience, there is no way I can be president.

*W*hat kind of experience do you think you need to run for office? Oh, gosh! I would need to really like it. Become hard and not too soft because they'll take advantage of you and then you would never make it. The Congress would probably take advantage of you or just the American people in general.

Special interest groups are the ones that will get you up there or not. If I want to be a politician ten or twenty years from now, if I'm going to have a ghost in my closet then forget it. Really, the mudslinging is so terrible right now, they'll get you. So I really have to start being real careful right now. Make sure I step in the right directions. Don't fool around, don't do anything illegal, don't inhale! [*Laughing*]

When I was in the seventh grade we had to do current events, and I thought: "I hate politics, I'll never understand politics." I did not know anything about it. It was just the mudslinging that was in my head. That's why I hated it so much. Now I understand enough to be able to make my decision on who I want to head this country. And now, I don't think politics is great, but it's a good thing. There is a lot of power behind those politicians; they have a lot of power.

*W*hat does the American dream mean to you? To me the American dream right now is college. My dream is doing what I want to do, what I feel in my heart that I want to do, being happy. I know that I am happy right now, but I can be a lot happier. That is my American dream—making it in the world. Beating the odds. Because there are enough odds against the minorities. In this country and with my values, I know I can beat the odds and make a difference.

I want to get into college, get my physician's assistant certificate, and I don't really want a family right after I graduate. I want a house. That is what I want; I want a house. Not a big, huge, elegant house—I want a house where I can be myself and decorate it the way I want it, wherever I want it. Because migrating and moving, I've moved five times. I could do that and buy me a real nice car or truck. And then probably like by the time I'm thirty, I might get married.

But I don't think I want a family now, not before I'm twenty-five or twenty-six. I really want my values straight before I can raise someone. Once you have a kid, he is yours forever. I do want to eventually raise a family, and especially in our culture, family is very important. My grandmother has twelve kids. But I also want to be able to provide for the family before I have a family. You know in today's world you see how a lot of marriages fail. That is why I'm looking—though I don't have kids yet—toward their future, what can happen if I end up a single mother or whatever, what it is going to do to them. And I want my kids to grow up happy. God first, then family, and then school. And then, if the right guy comes.

Do you think the country is moving in the right direction? Well right now, we're not because we are in the recession, I guess. I am a little depressed over that. Because the recession and so many people are unemployed, and that really affects me because my parents are often unemployed in the off-season. But we'll survive. The depression in the '30s, people had no hope at all. But the country survived that, and I think we can survive this recession. We'll get out of it, and we will keep on going. That's why it is so important for the adults to fix the mess that we are in. I think we're heading in the right direction. That is one of the great things about being an American—we can survive anything.

What do you think America will be like in fifty years? I hope there will be those cars that move in the air. The technology is going to be fantastic; maybe we will get to live on the moon. Maybe we will be able to reduce poverty and the homeless and the hungry. I can't wait. I am looking forward to it. If this pollution doesn't get us first. [*Laughing*] One thing I have is a lot of faith and hope. Everybody runs into problems, and the United States is not without problems. But I think we can survive them. If we all hope.

"Everything has its purpose."

Stanley J. Ritchie Jr.

The days are so full of work that they often last until the wee hours of the morning. The work is backbreaking at times and goes on rain or shine, in heat or in cold. The rewards: Lucky, a hand-raised pig who eagerly responds when called; a tobacco greenhouse built by hand; and 100 head of cattle winning top honors at local and national fairs. Growing up on a Frankfort, Kentucky, farm raising tobacco and Charolais cattle instilled in Stan Ritchie at an early age a love for farming. Now, this eighteen-year-old handles money by the tens of thousands of dollars, buying and selling cattle, tractors, and tobacco seedlings. He hopes to buy his own farm after he graduates from high school. With his busy schedule, Stan just manages to squeeze in the Rush Limbaugh show, hunting, and an occasional visit to his girlfriend in Colorado. For now, he just wants to keep on making a living off the land, saying, "I like things the way they are."

***W**hat has it been like to grow up on a farm?* I remember being out on the farm when I was four years old. That's the time I started driving tractors by myself. My mom was always fussing at my dad for having me out there, saying I was in the way.

I guess I enjoy it so much because I've been around it all my life. If I was raised up in the city, I don't know what my life would have been like, but it would have been totally different. The bad part about farm work is that you have to put in a lot of long hours, stay up until two or three in the morning during the summers. I guess I've just grown to love it. I can't stand to be inside very much; I'd rather be outside working in hay with the cattle or tobacco—except in the wintertime. In the wintertime, I about freeze to death.

I'd really like to run 200 head of cows and slowly but surely in the next two to five years I plan on having that. The tobacco side of it is a lot of labor if you raise 28,000 pounds like I'm doing. But that's just a drop in the bucket to some people here in the state. In Lexington, one person raised 750,000 pounds. In Kentucky as a whole, I'd say our farm would be be on the small size, but in Franklin County itself, I would call it a medium-size farm.

You have to have people who cut tobacco, load it on your wagons, and house it. But there's not enough help. People just don't want to work any more. They'd rather draw welfare, it seems like. Of course, now they've got tobacco-cutting machines, barns where you can hoist the tobacco with one person, and tobacco-stripping machines where you can strip an acre a day with one person, but all that costs a lot of money. You'd rather have the help there instead of just a machine that mixes it all up and doesn't separate it in grades as well as humans can.

Migrant workers help with the setting of the tobacco and during harvesting time, but you can't trust a lot of them. People recommend that you just let them do manual work and not drive tractors—it can be dangerous because you don't know what they're doing. You have to provide housing for them and food, and then [the loss] if they do try and steal anything, which is something that sometimes can happen when you hire people you don't know. That can be just about as expensive as if you have to go to the machine.

*H*ow are you able to handle such large blocks of time and sums of money so successfully? I don't mind working late. Sometimes during school, I'd just as soon stay up all night long if something needs to be done. I don't like to get up too awful early though because I'm not a morning person. I guess it's just a part of farming: you've got to be responsible for doing stuff and being places on time—which a lot of kids aren't able to do. It gets real hectic, especially during the summer. You take off school full time and then you don't get to see any of your

friends, except maybe on the road when you're going somewhere else. You just have to bring it to a halt and take a little time on a rainy day or something.

I guess handling money just comes along with it. I started saving up money in savings accounts when I was very young, and I bought my first cow when I was ten years old. Then I was keeping the calves and building up. Along the way, I was just trying good management. When you sell your tobacco crop, if you have 17,000 pounds, you get $1.83 a pound. But you've got to pay bills with it or keep it back for your expenses on next year's crop and labor and all that stuff. And if you go buy new equipment, nothing's cheap. A new tractor costs $28,500. That's a lot of money to stare at you in the face [*grinning*]. I paid $4,250 for that heifer for breeding purposes, to sell calves to other breeders in the registered Charolais business.

You can get FHA, Federal Home Administration loans, for the farm. While the regular interest was maybe 9, 10, 11 percent, the farm loans look like 5 percent. But not all banks are willing to go along with it. Hopefully, I'll be able to get one, but one of the drawbacks is if you already own a farm, you can't get an FHA loan. If I were buying my first farm through FHA, it would be all right.

Then if the tobacco industry goes out, what would you do, or if beef cattle prices go down, what are you going to use for your income? We have the cattle for the money, but tobacco is some farmers' only source of income besides little side jobs—without that they'd go bust.

If you look at tobacco, it's been around for years and years, people smoking, chewing, whatever. That's their right. On planes short distances or whatever where they have banned it, I guess that's all right because most people can survive, even if they are addicted to smoke. But look at how they are affected, such as people in a city or state job, or here in Frankfort, where state workers have to go to a designated room every time they want to smoke.

There are more than 62,000 tobacco farmers in the United States. Kentucky is second only to North Carolina in its total production of tobacco.

I personally don't believe the tobacco itself will hurt you. It may be the chemicals. Maybe they can take the chemical companies and make them design it where it isn't harmful. I think they've blown the danger out of proportion. If they want people not to be on unemployment, they better think about it before they destroy the tobacco industry. And really the tobacco companies are contributing to it themselves by going to South America. They've been building barns for these farmers down there—brand-new barns. The help down there is so much cheaper. That's where generic cigarettes are made.

When you buy generics for 80 cents to a dollar a pack and Marlboros for something like two dollars, people won't smoke ours. So we're cutting our own throats. They need to give us something else to grow. Some people say tobacco is going to be out in the next ten years. I am just kinda going along.

People will go to beef cattle, hogs, vegetables, or some other types of things to raise. But you can't raise too many, or there will be a big surplus of those and there won't be no money in that either. They're talking about Washington buying the farmers' poundage of tobacco, like milk, years ago.

If you go to beef cattle though, then you're worrying about people wanting to stop eating beef. But look at the protein and vitamins in beef. The body wasn't made to eat just all vegetables; it has to have that protein in there, the meat, calcium.

And if you don't eat that meat, people won't be able to sell cattle. If you knock out the tobacco *and* beef industry, you can't just dream up a job. Farmers have got to have money coming from something. You just ought to leave stuff the way it is.

***W**hat would you say to people who think raising animals on a farm is cruel?*
That's the way I'm making money. Raising them and selling them to eat. I've got hot shocks to shock them, but I only use them if I have a problem loading them when I'm selling them. If I'm keeping them on the farm for ten years, I won't use the shocks because I don't want them to get too wild or upset over it or every time they see me they'll want to run. But if I'm hauling calves off and they won't go, I'm going to shock them and I don't care who's in front of me or what. It's my animal, my property, and I have the right to do it. I just don't see how other people can get upset over it, as long as you're not really hurting the animals.

Some environmental people have gone in the woods during deer season, and they'll follow you around so you can't get any deer. If anybody ever came on my place like that, I'd give them a warning that they're trespassing. And [*jokingly*] if they still do that, you scare the living daylights out of them, and then probably go to jail! If they want to protest, get a permit, go to the state capitol or county courthouse; don't be coming on people's land! All they're doing is making more enemies instead of trying to get people on their side. There are some people who would probably just as soon try and shoot them.

God put animals here for a purpose. That's the way to look at it. I mean, everything has its purpose. Their purpose is to provide food for humans. They produce the young so they keep themselves populated, and when they repopulate themselves to the point where the cows are too old, you take the heifer and replace it. Let her have ten or eleven years of work in a herd, and then they eventually go on into hamburger.

*D*o you ever get attached to any of your farm animals? Yeah, you can get attached to just about anything. I've got a horse a year and three months older than me, and I wouldn't sell it for the world! You take animals like that bull and heifer I paid so much for, and you get financially attached, but I can pretty much take out anything that I have to, to sell or kill or whatever. Also, if something got hurt and I wanted to try and keep it alive but I know I'm hurting it more, I'd rather kill it. Like pulling the plug on somebody in the bed wanting to die but they keep machines going to keep them alive. You got to look at it from two different perspectives.

*W*hat do you think about the environment? The Sierra Club, they've got a lot of stuff they would like to change. If you own land that borders a river, they want to be able to come on our land anytime they want. They don't want you to mow any of the grass; they want it to all go back to the way of nature!

You can't just let all that grow up. [There's no need to] stop some of the tree cutting because it's replenishing itself. It's just like in trees that we log out, we turn around and there are little sprouts coming right back up for a second growth. I don't believe there is any danger of running out of trees for oxygen or whatever.

I don't know how much cleaning up on the bays or whatever we should do—the companies who did it should be helping clean up, just like Exxon when they had the tanker get a hole and leak all that oil. They're the ones with the money; we're not. So if there are companies they know are responsible for syringes or whatever it is coming up on the bay, maybe they ought to be the ones to clean up, because I'm sure we've got better things we could waste our time and money on.

*W*ith the demands on your time, have you been tempted to just drop out of school and work? There wasn't really any temptation to drop out, but a lot of times you think that if there is something that needs to be done, you're gonna miss a day of school, and they only give you five days per school year to miss for tobacco farming. And that's not enough time, usually. So you have to take sick days or something. If you show cattle, you've got to miss school because some shows will be on a Thursday or Friday or be two or three states away. Then you go and if you miss ten days, you've got to realize, "How much more school can I afford to miss?" So, you weigh the two evils and go with the better one. Of course it's bad to miss school. You're going to miss something that one day of school that you would have needed. I don't think there's anything about farming that would make me quit school.

I plan to at least graduate from high school and take some college classes, but I probably won't be going to full-time college. I couldn't afford to, timewise. It's not the money. I could get agricultural scholarships with the awards and stuff I've gotten and it wouldn't cost very much. It's just time—the time if I miss farming compared with the money I could make.

*W*hat does FFA stand for? It used to stand for the Future Farmers of America. Now it's more than just a bunch of farmers. You have got a lot of girls in it now and you don't have just the country people; you've got city people in it also. You meet here at the school, have projects, go to contests, and try to further your knowledge about anything from flowers to swine. We have around seventy members, maybe an average-sized club. I don't know if you can really call it Future Farmers; it's more like the

> In 1820, farm jobs comprised nearly 72 percent of the total number of jobs in the United States. Today, they comprise just 2.4 percent.

agribusiness, agriculture, sort of future agriculturalists. I'm a treasurer. I was last year and am again this year. I keep the bills we pay and money we receive from fundraisers.

A lot of times people look on farmers or FFA as just a bunch of hicks. They know who we are and most of the time we come fairly decent dressed, but every once in awhile, if I have to, I'll wear my farm boots, if I've got something to do after school. It's nothing that bad. People may not like it, but there's not much they can do about it. We just kind of overlook them, or we look at it as an ignorance in that they don't really know what they are talking about.

Some people will call you rich. A lot of people think that "well if you've got this, that, and the other," you must have more money. I'm nowhere near it. What I make is to spend. It's just a revolving cycle. Sure I make this money, but you don't pay the bills I pay each month. And so really you don't have that much to play with when it's all done. And then a lot of kids come up and say, "I ain't got no lunch money, give me some money." A lot of people who do that have jobs and just don't want to take the steps to make sure they have money. You've got to know who your friends are if you want to lend money out and just kind of walk on by the other ones. It may be mean but you can't afford to give everybody stuff. I can't.

How do you think the country as a whole is doing on issues of discrimination and racism? I'd say it's according to where you go in the United States. I know in the South there's still some conflict about it. You have your old people that are never going to change—they were brought up saying it and that's how they're going to say it till the day they die. A good example of that was A.B. Chandler, the governor of Kentucky. He was a real big supporter of the University of Kentucky Wildcats and because he let a word slip in one of the Board of Directors' meetings, they tried to run him off the Board.

What word? Nigger. That's the way he was brought up and he didn't care who was around. It's just according to where you go, I guess. Around this area I guess things are about the same, maybe getting a little bit better. I don't think they're any worse. For the most part, people get along. A lot of people can put racism aside and just go ahead and talk and help your neighbor if they need help.

I've heard that there's still a Ku Klux Klan in Frankfort. Do you know anything about that? Well, in Frankfort itself, there is not really a Klan. There was at one time a proposal to get a Klan together, but I don't believe they've ever come through. So, it's said there's still a Klan organization in neighboring counties and some people think it's good and some say nobody should belong to it. But the Klan has really changed from the old days or at least according to what I've read or been told. Now it's illegal for the Klan to wear hoods or anything like this. It's freedom of speech as long as they're not really hurting anybody. And as far as I know, lately they're not. But some people say it still doesn't matter, that the Klan is a group of white people that believes certain things. But then you look and you have the NAACP and that's a group of black people and to me it's not really a whole lot of difference in it.

The Klan is still for the rights of white people. It seems like according to them that white people are starting to diminish to a point where they need to start coming back. The NAACP is for the black people. That's for civil rights or more job opportunities, but yet there's nothing wrong with that. It just tears me up to see one thing not allowed, and then they let other people have their own little groups. So it's a really hard situation to try to sort out, is it good or bad? If somebody asks you to join it, would you want to or not? You never really know.

Have you had any personal experiences with racism or the Klan? I was over in Lawrenceburg on the day that the Los Angeles policemen were acquitted and the riots broke out, and for some reason or another, the black people there decided I was going to be a victim of that. I don't know how they could know me or if they knew me or they just picked me randomly. As I was coming through downtown late at night, they pulled out in front of me in two cars and jumped out with sticks in their hands, and started yelling a bunch of stuff like "You're gonna get it." And so I backed the tractor trailer up through downtown Lawrenceburg and was scared half to death since I didn't have no protection with me. All of a sudden, somebody from behind me pulled up and jumped out. I thought I was in for it then, but they started yelling slurs and told the blacks if they wanted to mess with somebody, to mess with them. Sure enough they left. They apparently didn't want to get in a big fight. I guess it was all right four on one, but when they had four on two, or maybe three, they didn't want to have nothing on. There never was anything out of it; they just tore out and never was seen again, but it still scared me half to death.

It made me think a lot before I get in a situation or if I'm around a bunch of people, black people in particular where they start talking about stuff or somebody comes up and starts messing around. I didn't get hurt so I was lucky. That's life. I guess you've got to go on and live with it. You can't let it hold you down. It may have been different if I had gotten hurt or something. [*Pause*] I'd say if I had gotten hurt, my dad would have been out looking for somebody.

*T**here is a lot of criticism of teenagers for not really knowing about what's going on in the country. How do you feel about that?*** I don't know where they go to get those type of statistics. For the most part, people around here seem to know what's going on. Of course we have Channel One in school every morning. It tells you from different points of view what's going on—if you pay attention. [*Grinning*] If you are alert to what you see in newspapers, on the news at home, or in the mornings here at school, you pretty well have got to know what's going on unless you just have no interest in it. I don't think they ought to count that against teenagers.

*H**ow would you describe what the government does?*** Give themselves a whole lot of extra money! I think they could cut out a lot of spending and stuff. A lot of people don't keep near the promises they say they are going to, especially when they are Democrats trying to get elected. [*Grinning*] I think they want to help some people—for instance, helping farmers out—and there are some people there who don't want to do nothing for us.

They could quit making so much stuff overseas. It might cost a little more, but it would be better to have Americans working.. It also seems like the United States gets involved in too much. A little country gets into trouble and we've got to be the rescuer. I think sometimes we kind of poke our nose where it don't belong. The people that are starving, I guess, in Bosnia and over in Africa and stuff, they've got some bad problems; I'm sure people feel for them. But to send a bunch of Americans over there—if they had gotten shot, that is kind of a waste of life. I don't think we really need to be over there. The United Nations could have done something as a whole, but there were more Americans over there, I think, than anything else. So we need to cut down, stay at home, and keep our interests to ourselves.

The government seems to waste a lot of money. It seems like everything is going up, up, up, never a down side to it. I don't know if that's ever going to change. It's so few people and so much power. Sometimes I wonder if we'd be better off if we had a president that made the rules and not a Congress.

*I*f you could change one thing about the government, what would it be? [*Long pause*] I would stop people in government from raising their pay that they get every year or every two years. I don't see how that job can be worth that much money. It just seems like every once in awhile, there was a ten- or twenty-thousand dollar payment that they would receive. I don't know if they have gotten one recently or not. They could take that money and put it towards something better, whether it be the deficit or new crops for us to grow when they take our tobacco away. I just think it's a big waste of taxpayers' money—put it to better use.

I guess the main problems I've had with our system of government are in things like the L.A. riots last year. They had the trial again and they went ahead and convicted Sergeant Koon and Officer Powell. I believe the main reason was because they didn't want another riot. You shouldn't convict those people and ruin their lives forever or possibly make them go broke through fines just to keep down a riot.

*D*o you consider yourself a Republican? Pretty much. I guess about nine times out of ten I would think.

*A*nd you listen to Rush Limbaugh? Oh yeah, gotta listen to Rush!

*W*hat did you think of the election? I guess Ross Perot hurt Bush and took some of his votes. I would have rather seen Bush stay in there.

But you have to go on with it. I think we're a hundred and some days into America held hostage! [*Laughter*]

*O*h yeah? Is that a Rush Limbaugh saying? You got it! [*Grinning*] Every time his show comes on, they sit there and they show the White House and the peace sign, and sometimes a little picture of somebody smoking grass, and Ross Perot up in the corner sitting there with his ears wiggling back and forth. And it says, "America held hostage," and whatever, if it's been 115 days since the election, whenever Clinton took office. It's kind of unusual to sit there and watch it.

I don't know if we're held hostage or not. I mean, I kind of figure we'll be worse off by the time this four years are up than we were. I don't think we were so bad and needing a jump start in our economy and this, that, and the other when he took over. It seemed all the news reporters were going for Clinton and putting everybody down on Bush. The media hurt Bush. They kept him out of there. They never seem to show both sides. I take the news with a grain of salt.

*W*hat do you think of the family-values debate when Vice President Dan Quayle was criticizing Murphy Brown for being a single mother? Well, I believe he was 100 percent right, but a lot of people disagree with that. Of course they show all this brutal killing on TV, and people act like they don't care anymore. You could be a five-year-old watching it or a fifty-year-old. It would be a lot better if it said "parental discretion" before you watch the movie. And if you've got the cable channels, who knows what you'll see on that. A lot of TV shows single mothers or one-night stands and then going on about your business the next day. That's pretty much what he was talking about and I think he was right.

I'd say there should be a certain limit to what's shown on regular public television. Seems like there is more and more violence, cussing, and everything else on there. I think they ought to do something about it. What? I don't know.

Some of the problems come from the parents where they don't care, like that story where parents left the kids and went on vacation.

Leaving two young kids, they must be crazy or something! And then, I heard something about last night it seemed like a lady hung her baby, tied it to the attic ceiling. I don't know what, but they ought to do something to her. If you don't want the kids, you ought to watch what you do and not have the kids. Don't be bringing another child into the world. It seems like there are not very many morals or family morals.

What role does the church play in your life? It plays a fairly important role. I've always been brought up in church although for a while I quit going, started staying at home and going out and doing anything but going to church. But you see signs, you know? We used to not do anything on Sundays, but I used the bulldozer one afternoon, and then the rain let out. And I couldn't use it at all. It makes you wonder: coincidence? Or is it somebody trying to tell you something—like stay in the house!

Who are your heros? I guess I'd have to go for my father. He has a way of doing things by himself and really putting in the long hours. Most people want to quit when dark time comes, whether it needs to be done or not. If there's something that he wants to get done, he don't care if it takes to the next morning.

What is your idea of a good citizen? You ought to be active, recycling, keeping around you clean, working, and maybe taking care of your family—not just being dope smokers, hippies, and whatever, sitting there doing nothing! I think that you need to have a good attitude and pay taxes.

How about voting? Is that part of that? Yeah, if you got the right to vote, you might as well vote. But if you don't want to take the time to stay registered, you may as well stay out of it. If you are not qualified, you shouldn't go vote, but you ought to try to see who you think would be the best out of all of the candidates.

***W**hat is the most valuable right to you?* Freedom. Being able to go just anywhere you want to go, being able to hold a job, unless they see you have committed a crime. A lot of people don't have that right of freedom. You don't realize it until you see somebody on TV and you realize what you've got and you think about it—*a lot.*

***W**hat's your "American dream"?* [*Pause*] I guess it would have to do with farming—trying to have a farm if possible and having everything I want on it. Having stuff paid for, making money, not having to worry about paying out to everybody and everything. Living, not maybe well off, but living where you're not really hurting. I guess that'd be the most I would ask for.

"We're all people."

Anitra S Washington

Like many southern youth, seventeen-year-old Anitra Washington responds to adults' questions with a polite "yes, ma'am" or "no, sir." But beneath her gracious manner is a highly motivated, self-confident fighter determined to be successful in her career and her life. Anitra lives with her mother and three younger brothers in the countryside outside the small southern Georgia town of Vienna. She studies hard, loves to read, especially black history, and enjoys spending time with her boyfriend when he is home on leave from the Army. A member of her high school's Junior ROTC and senior class president, Anitra believes passionately that good planning and hard work will lead to achieving her goals. "I'm gonna speak my mind no matter what," she says proudly. "If I'm not speaking my opinion, I'm not being myself, and I like being me!"

Tell me about your experience with Junior ROTC. I'm a cadet PFC—that's Private First Class. I'm in the color guard. We carry rifles, the state flag, the United States flag, and the ROTC flag. We do trips to competitions or for field trips. Every sixth week, we have a cookout or a little get-together.

In our classes, we discuss American history. On Mondays, we discuss World War I and II, and we have quizzes on it. We have a workbook and a lecture-activity book. For me, it's a repeat of U.S. history and civics. We do map reading and learn to use a compass. At first it was kind of difficult, but it's okay now; I got the hang of it.

On Wednesday, we have drill and ceremony—that's when we do drill with our weapon. Then we play knockout. In that, our leader calls us to attention and after that command, everything else has to be done correctly. If you mess up, he'll call you out and say, "All right, knock 'em out." That's five push-ups. Everyone tries not to get out because they don't want to do those push-ups. [*Laughs*] In knockout, you want to laugh at the people, but if you laugh, you've got to knock 'em out too. So you have to be serious.

> Approximately 126,000 students participate nationwide in the U.S. Army's Junior ROTC. Of those, 40 percent are white, 41 percent black, 14 percent Hispanic, and 5 percent other. Around 27 percent of Junior ROTC members go on active duty, and another 9 percent enter the Reserves or National Guard.

On Fridays, we do exercises for about five or ten minutes and then we play volleyball. Sometimes we'll do a cadet's challenge. That's where a certain age group has to do a certain number of pushups, pull-ups, running a mile, obstacle time. It's fun though.

We get merits for the good things we do, like working at concession stands, being on time, volunteering, winning knockouts. You can get demerits for things like being late for class or chewing gum in the classroom or on the rifle range.

I sort of got in ROTC by accident. My uncle had been persuading me, but I'd heard that the National Guard colonel in charge was a mean kind of guy, and I was like, un-uh, I can't take it. Then this year, my schedule got mixed up, and that was the only thing open for fifth period, so I said, "I guess I'll try it." And I got in, and I liked it! It's fun. We do mostly everything the Army does—except get up early in the morning! [*Laughing*]

*H*ow has this experience changed you? It teaches me to have more respect for myself and to have respect for my peers as well as my elders. Since being in ROTC, I respect people under me as well. Also, it teaches discipline. There are a lot of things we can't do and say out there because we'll get demerits. It teaches me to be a better American—to value my citizenship more and myself as a human being.

If I had it to do over again, I would go in earlier, so I would have higher rank. Then I could be the head of my class, call roll, get everyone to stand at attention, and do the pledge of allegiance.

*H*ow would you describe the rights and responsibilities of being an American citizen? It's like, basically, being able to do what you choose. You have a right to do certain things that you wouldn't have in other countries. Here, you have freedom of choice, freedom of religion, freedom of speech, to a certain extent. I'm proud to be an American because I can choose my friends, my religion, my goals in life. In other countries, I would have to do what the government says I must do [as a career], like be a factory worker. Here I have to follow the government's rules, but I can choose my own job and buy what I want to buy, whenever I want to buy it. That's what being an American citizen means to me—having my freedom.

We must also obey the law. We must defend our country whenever we are called. We have a responsibility to vote. We must voice our opinion. You don't have any say-so in the government if you don't voice your opinion and vote; you're like the silent majority. I'm seventeen now, and I'm looking forward to voting in my first election.

Some people say that your generation is not really interested in politics and government. Do you agree? No, I really don't. All of the people in my school were interested in who was to become our next president and vice president. We even had a mock election at school. The majority voted for Clinton. He won at our school, and he won overall!

In civics, we did reports about politics, reports about the electors. When we first started off, last year, we were kind of puzzled because [David] Duke was running and everybody knew that he was KKK, and all of us blacks were saying, "If he wins, we're catching the boat for Jamaica 'cause we ain't pickin' no cotton." [*Laughs*] That's just a stereotype; we were just saying that as a joke. But, in a way, I was kind of scared.

Not all of my classmates were interested in the election. The ones that are the most involved [in class discussions] and ask questions, we were the most interested. The ones that sat around just listening, they really didn't care. They'd say they want someone to win and leave it at that.

The mock election was fun. We have the Channel One program that comes on every morning in homeroom, and they were sponsoring it. We would check who we wanted on a ballot and give it to the homeroom teacher. In the ballot was a ticket for a free Whopper. Everybody wanted to get that!

But even without that incentive, we would have still done it because we were interested. I think this election was like when Hoover was president. Hoover got the blame for the Great Depression, and now that the economy is down—Bush, like everything is on him. I think that's one reason Clinton won, because of the downslide in the economy.

On election night, I was very happy. Everybody was looking at the television and saying to me, "Will you shut up?!" I was like glued to the set, and they were like, "The Braves game is on," and I said, "Forget the Braves; we've got to look at this!" Then when Clinton won, I went just wild! I was just jumping. I was very happy. A change is coming!

*W*hat are some of the things you think he'll change? For one thing, he'll change gays in the military. We discussed it at school. The teacher asked some of the guys if they'd want to be in close quarters with gays, and they were like no, because if you were in close quarters and they'd accidentally touch you, that would bother them. We were debating about it, and the teacher would say, "But what if you were gay? You'd want your representation and your job." I say they're human just like we're human, and they deserve a chance.

Clinton's for the American people all the way; he's for the minority and the majority as well. I feel that he's going to be a great president because all of the other presidents have always come from a wealthy family and he didn't come from a wealthy family. He knows what it feels like to be down and out, so he understands the problems of the American people, middle-class and lower-class and working people.

*W*hat did you think about the campaign? I felt that, with all the candidates, you couldn't trust no one, because everyone was saying this person was lying and that person was lying and how did you know your candidate wasn't lying? Who do you trust? 'Cause people were saying, don't trust this guy, don't trust that guy. People will do anything for a vote, just about.

*D*id you feel that way about Clinton, too, even though you were for him? In a way I did. None of the candidates were just saying "I'm for this"; they'd say, "Look at what the others did." They should show both sides of it. I watched all of the debates. Some of it made me mad because they were digging in Clinton's personal files, and I felt that's not their business. But that's politics—they're going to do that.

*W*hat do you think are the biggest problems in the country? The AIDS epidemic. People didn't think AIDS was a big issue until superstars got it. I guess they thought they were incapable of getting it, but now they know anyone can get it.

There's also racism, but I know we can't do anything about racism because that's within a person; we can't make a person change. A small child will do whatever its parents do, and when they see their parents treat other people wrong because of their race, they're going to say, "If mama does it, I'll do it too." If you try to change them while they're young, it might work out, but once they get into their teens and older, it's going to take a lot—you can't hardly change it.

My friends and I once went into a store to do some shopping, and there was a white cashier. Well, she stopped working and went to watching us. I wanted to say, "We don't steal, we're respectable teenagers!" We were going to spend our money in that shop, about eight of us, but we decided we didn't want to shop there with somebody watching us all the time. We went to another store, and she didn't get a sale. I told my aunt about it—she has a store—and she said there was a high crime rate in that area and a lot of people come in there to steal, so that's why the cashier was being so aware. I understand that. But we didn't come there to steal; we came there to spend our money. I just feel some white people see a black person and think they're going to steal, but then a white person can come in and rob them blind while they're watching us!

I don't think any of my classmates are racist. We all get along. We can sit down and have a great conversation. I got in a fight with a white girl once, but we were back together the next day because we were good friends. I don't have just a specific group I socialize with.

Also, our school has two homecoming queens, one white and one black. Some wanted to change it to just one, but I felt we couldn't change it. It's been there ever since we've been integrated. It wouldn't be fair to the white persons because there's a majority of black persons at our school, so the queen would always be black. Even if the person the white students picked wasn't good for the job, they should still be able to pick one. If we just had one, with the white students being in the minority, they wouldn't have as much say-so. So we've got to keep it. It's separate but equal.

*A*re there just blacks and whites in your school? Are there other ethnic groups? Blacks, whites, Hispanics, Indians [from India]. That's about it. There are some Hispanic students who ride our bus, and they don't speak English that well. I went up to one girl and said, "How do you do, what's your name?" She tried to say, "No speak English," but I didn't hear her. I just kept on talking to her, and she said, "No speak English." Then, I said, "Oh, I'm sorry," and I asked another Hispanic student, "How do you say 'I'm sorry' in Spanish?" They get along okay in school because there are some Mexicans there who can speak English and Spanish as well. And our French teacher also speaks Spanish. Whenever someone new comes to the school, we try to make them feel welcome—at least I do—ask them what their name is—let them know they have a friend there.

Tell me about your summer job as a library assistant. I got the job as part of the JTPA program—Job Training Partnership of America. They'll find you a job. The job was kind of difficult because you have to learn the Dewey decimal system, and the librarian didn't want someone who didn't know it. So I came home and learned it that night, and I went back the next day and got the job.

I've done it for two summers. I do research for people that call in. I put up books, keep the library tidy. I started a black history file, so when people come in February [Black History Month] and ask for black authors, they can just pull the file out. They're really useful books, some written by slaves and by Paul Lawrence Dunbar. We had to take every book off the shelf and look at them because you couldn't always tell by the title if it was about black history. It could be about building ships, but it would fit in anyway if it had something to do with slavery or black history. Then we had to do the elementary section and do the same thing. But that was easier because pictures were on the front of the book! [*Laughs*]

The people that come there are basically pretty nice, but some of them are set in their old ways. If they see a black person, they expect you to wait on them hand and feet. At the copy machine, they bring you the money, and they say, "I want five copies." And I say in a nice way, "I'll show you how to work it—it's coin-operated, but that's not my job to do it for you."

Why do you say you enjoy studying American history? In history, every day you always learn something new. Things you never dreamed about happening are there in history! I like discussing the Hoover days, the Great Depression, the period after the Revolution. It does puzzle me that some history books have only one section on black history. When we get to college, there's going to be some stuff about black history they'll ask us and we've never been exposed to it. That's why I want to teach history, so I can cover all cultures and all races and all ethnicities. You need to give all people the chance to learn about their own origin and their race because there are a lot of famous Latinos and a lot of famous black Americans and a lot of famous Jews that people need to learn more about. We often just hear about famous white men. That's not bad, but we should be exposed to more than just that.

You benefit from learning about history because a lot of what's already happened is happening over again. You benefit from learning about heroes because you learn they were people just like you that had goals and dreams, and they had to have a hero, someone who helped them climb the ladder to success. You can say, look at them, he did it or she did it, and they came from a poor background, so you can do it also! It's inspirational.

*W*ho are your heroes? My heroes are Mr. Rackard, my civics teacher; my mother; and myself. I'm my own hero! [*Laughs*] My mother tells me every day to make something out of myself, go to school, get a good education, be successful—just don't go to school and stop. Mr. Rackard is a role model to the whole senior class because he tells you every day that he wants you to know your rights as an American citizen. That way, if you're in a court case or you're on a jury, you won't be so puzzled about what they're talking about. We all have rights and responsibilities as citizens, but a lot don't know about them.

*D*o you think our system of government works? Yes, it works to a certain extent. It works unless you get a corrupt person in office. It might not always work when you want it, but it works. Just like in the legal system for a trial, you can get your trial appealed. In some countries, you might not be able to do that. You'd be put in jail to rot. We're given a lawyer if you can't afford one, whereas in other countries, if you can't afford it, tough luck.

*W*hat are your most cherished rights as an American? I value the most the First Amendment, freedom of expression; the Twenty-sixth, the right to vote; the Thirteenth, Fourteenth, Fifteenth, the civil rights amendments. If we hadn't had those civil rights amendments, we wouldn't be able to voice our opinion. We as black people wouldn't have the rights of citizens; we'd still be treated as property.

*D*o you trust politicians? No. Because they can lie so good it seems like it's the truth. The only politicians I respect are Jesse Jackson, President-elect Bill Clinton, and Wyche Fowler [former U.S. Senator from Georgia]. That's about it. I met Mr. Fowler about a month ago. We had a groundbreaking ceremony here, and the senior class went and we met him and shook his hand and he seemed like a very nice guy.

*D*o you know many women who are in politics? I don't really know them by name; I know their faces. They are new to me. I know Sandra Day O'Connor, because she's the only woman on the Supreme Court.

It's not a good idea to have too many women in govern-ment because a woman has the heart. She's sympathet-ic. Some of them that are not strong can fall for anything. Whereas a man is set in his ways, and if he says no, he won't be too much persuaded to change his mind. He thinks about a lot of important issues at a different angle to how a woman sees it. He may have a woman adviser; that helps him out.

I feel there should be some minorities in government so their culture and background can have a voice in government as well.

*W*ould you like to run for office someday? I wouldn't mind being like a senator or representative; they have a pretty smooth job. But not president or governor—too much is focused on that one person in those jobs. If something goes wrong, everything's on you!

*W*hat does the phrase "the American dream" mean to you? For me, the American dream means for people to pursue their goals in life, and to have respect for themselves and others, and to have their rights as well. And just to be free. Don't go wild, but be free—and respect the government.

For me personally, I plan to enter the National Guard in the summer. In school in the fall, at Albany State College, I want to take up history, and teach it at the high school level. But I want to take up culinary arts as a hobby on the side, so when school is out in the summer, I'll have something to keep me busy. I like to cook. I wouldn't mind catering because there will always be parties and get-togethers and weddings, and if you do the job right, people will respect you and come to your business.

I don't want to do this around here. Maybe in New York, I probably could do okay. You can't make a living around here; it's too hard to pull yourself up.

*Y*ou want to be in the National Guard, and you have relatives and friends who are in the military. What are your feelings about the military in general? A lot of people say that recruiters just tell you good things to get you signed up; it's not all what they make it. But people who have gone in and came out say they enjoyed it. I feel that the military disciplines you. It teaches you to have honor and love and respect for your country. It matures you. You go in as a wild teenager and you come out as a young man or a young lady to have respect for themselves and for others. It's like a meditation period, because you're away from things that try to hold you back. You get a chance to meet different people and you get a chance to travel and you have a little fun and you get in shape. I just want to go into the National Guard for the experience.

If you could change anything about American government, what would it be?
The unfairness of the government. The government's not fair; it's not just. People say that black people are the causes of a lot of drugs and weapons—what puzzles me is that we don't have any planes to bring that stuff in! When they have a big drug bust, they don't never get the big guy; they just get the little guy.

It makes me mad to see a black person get so drunk on the corner they don't know what's going on. That person could have been anything he or she wanted to be, but they got this habit and the habit brought them down. It's sickening because people of other races see him and turn their nose up. I'm mad at the person because he should better himself. He doesn't have to live that way.

As far as other government policies, we need to pay the debt that the government owes. Also, this welfare thing: people that are eligible to work and don't have anything wrong with them sit home every day, have babies, and get a check. People down the road are living good, they don't have a worry in the world, and they're getting their check to stay home. They don't clean up; they don't cook for their kids; they just sit around with that television. Their kids eat sandwiches every day or they don't even eat. I mean even if they go out and try to get a job, they get more from the check. So what's the incentive? It burns me up. Whereas my mother is a single parent and she tries to get help for us and they won't help her. My mother's struggling, but we're gonna' have everything that we need—a decent dinner every night, and my mother has her bills paid and all that.

I get real satisfaction from working and doing things for myself. I just don't want to be somebody's housewife. I want to be able to work and make my own money and be independent by myself because I'm the only one that can help me. I'm going to make something out of myself because I don't want to be sitting home waiting on no check! I want my own check that I've made, that I've worked for.

*W*hat do you think America will be like in fifty years? [*Laughs*] I really don't know. I never really thought about it. I hope there won't be any more drugs in society because with all the drugs going around, just about anybody can get them and sell them.

It may be better. With the new president, he may try to make it work. But with more and more hate groups coming out—like the Nazis starting again [in Germany]—I say, please don't come over here with that. In Atlanta, a lot of whites have moved from the inner-city. It's sickening because the black race is killing their own selves. You don't see many Mexicans, whites, Jews, killing themselves or their family but you see violence in the cities with blacks.

I do feel that a lot of the racial issues have changed with the younger people. You cannot change the older heads. But the younger people are being brought up now being together. Whereas my grandmother, your grandparents, they were separated. My mother went to segregated schools until her first year of high school when they were integrated. Now it's common for interracial marriages; it's common for black and white people to play together.

I just wish that the world would come together and put all the color behind us. In school, I sometimes say to people, "Will you stop with this black girl, white girl thing? Let's quit with that. We're all people. We're all people." We're all the same because we've got a heart. It's the heart; it's not the color of your skin. It's the person inside you. And if people could get around that, we'd be a better society. That's the way I see it.

"I just don't think there is enough effort."

Sylvia Flute

Seventeen-year-old Sylvia Flute belongs to the Lower Brule tribe of the Sioux nation. She lives on a scenic reservation near the sparkling blue Missouri River in central South Dakota with her parents and six siblings. Native American culture plays a big role in her life, but she wants people to know Indians don't live in tipis or travel by horse-drawn wagons anymore. Sylvia lives in a small comfortable ranch house and attends school on the reservation. The reservation is still predominantly agricultural, with its own herds of buffalo and elk. But it is also predominantly poor, and many residents have alcohol problems. The tribal council of the reservation recently tried to improve its standard of living by opening a gambling casino. For now, Sylvia hopes to be the first in her family to attend college, after which she wants to find ways to improve the quality of life on the reservation and to preserve her Native American Lakota culture.

*H*ow would you describe South Dakota? It's all plateaus, few trees, a lot of flat land all over. You don't see smog anywhere, not even in Rapid City. It's really beautiful. When I was in New Jersey, I couldn't see nothing; there were trees everywhere! Here I can see houses, hills, just the open air and the river. I can't stand to be in other places.

The people I met in New Jersey would say, "You really an Indian?" They asked my mom a bunch of questions about the reservation and South Dakota. When they found out we don't live in tipis or anything anymore, they were surprised! They thought the stuff was interesting.

At times it's kind of hard being Native American because of some of the prejudice around. People just don't accept you for who you are, and they always judge you and stuff. If they were in our shoes, then they'd know how we felt whenever they say stuff to us. But I like being Native American. It's fun. There are a lot of different things for us to do, like go to powwows and different gatherings. We have big families, so somebody will always be there for us. I think Native Americans are special, because Caucasians don't have no heritage or nothing to fall back on, while we have all different kinds. We have the Lakota and Sioux language and culture. I want to learn my language. I feel weird because most of my friends don't speak Lakota. I don't know if they want to or not, but I'm one of the ones that wants to. I think it will help out, and then I can teach my kids. I think it's better being a Native American.

*W*hat are your favorite cultural traditions? The food. I like the food. The fry bread and the wojapi [fruit pudding]. We have other kinds of food, but just smelling them turns me off. I've tried tripe; it's like liver. My grandma makes it every summer and you walk into her house and then have to go back out. The smell!

I would probably also say the powwows are my favorite. There are different powwows all over South Dakota, and in Montana and North Dakota. A powwow is a gathering of different tribes. We have a powwow every year here on our reservation in August. A lot of tourists come. It's usually three days long.

One of the big activities at a powwow is dancing. We have different categories of dancing. There is the women's traditional, women's fancy, and women's jingo. Then there is men's traditional, men's grass, and men's fancy. My brother is a fancy dancer. We usually have dancing contests in those six categories.

And we have a bunch of different concession stands where we have different kinds of food. Everybody comes to either dance or watch. It's like our local fair. We have baseball and softball tournaments going on and a rodeo during that time.

If you had to choose between being a citizen of the Sioux nation and being a U.S. citizen, which would you choose? My Sioux nation. I have a lot of ancestors that I look up to who fought in wars and stuff. I want to try and accomplish as much as they did. I would also choose my Sioux nation because we have such big families and our cultures will always be there. I can always fall back on that stuff. If I chose the other one, what can I fall back on?

My grandpa is a medicine man. I don't know how old he is, but he lived here all his life. My uncle is going to sweats [sweat lodges] right now with him. The sweats are when you go in a hut with fire going inside and it's really hot. You just sit there and pray. You talk with whoever is in there. It's usually medicine men, but a lot of people go for different reasons. I think they have them every weekend. It's a form of church. We just sweat and sweat and sweat. My grandpa built one himself.

We are enrolled in the Episcopal Church, but most of my family goes to the sweat. Only once in a while do we go down to church, for Christmas or Easter or something like that.

I've never been in a sweat before. I don't think any of us kids have except my brother. He had to go through sweat before he got his Indian name. He would go every weekend. You just go as much as you can before you get your name, and then during a name-giving ceremony, they have one of the older relatives come and give you an Indian name. You can be any age when you get your name.

***D*o you have one?** No, I don't. I want one! I don't know if my mom is planning on it or not. There is a lot of planning that goes into it. You have to have a feed and a giveaway. A feed is when you feed everybody that's there, make a big old dinner. In the giveaways, you have to buy gifts, like a pair of socks or something, and pass them out to everybody. On the days we have giveaways during the powwow, whoever is in the arena gets something. We also had star quilts made and they were given to my grandparents for my brother's giveaway. That's the way to say thank you to your family.

It's very interesting to go to a powwow and see what's really there. If I was a different race, I would be like, "What are you talking about?" I would be so confused. But since I'm Native American, I know how it is. It's kind of hard to explain to people until they go and see for themselves.

***W*hat kind of experience have you had with prejudice?** Not much. But in one instance, we got kicked out of a store. It was an Honors Night party, and we went to Chamberlain. We got done eating, and we all went into a store. Most of us came out and got on a bus, but a couple of kids went back in because they forgot somethin'. The manager came out and said, "Sorry, we're closed." But it was only seven o'clock, and they don't close till nine. They even called the cops. They thought we were stealing. It got everybody all ticked off, and we told our local papers. After that, the manager of the store came down and apologized, but I think everybody had a lot of questions that he couldn't answer, like why he did that.

Things like that really get me mad. After that happened I didn't want to go back into that store. He lost a lot of business for that.

I think we [Native Americans] all work as one. Once one of us gets in trouble or something happens to us, the whole town knows and then we all stay behind each other. It's not easy, but we have to deal with it, and have to see it as hard being Native American because of prejudice—a lot of people not liking us just because they think we are trying to steal land or something from them.

***W*here do they get those ideas?** I have no idea!

*W*hat do you think would help stop the prejudice and misunderstanding? If we go around and talk, then other races will know what we're going through. We need to let them know how we feel when this stuff happens to us. It's not that complicated, just to come in and listen. At a seminar we had on Wounded Knee, all I seen there was Indians, just all Native Americans. This one girl commented that, "If the whites want to know how we live and how we grew up, how come I don't see none in here?"

I think there is enough interest; I just don't think there is enough effort.

*H*ow is the Sioux Nation different from others? Well, I don't think the Sioux Nation is very much different from anything. We're just one of many different tribes from all over and we all have our own language and our own cultures, but I don't think we are different from anyone else.

As for Lower Brule, I don't think we're very different, except this is supposed to be a dry reservation [no alcohol]. What really got everyone mad here is because they put a bar in there [at the new casino]. I don't think Brule is any different from anywhere else except for the casino.

I don't like the casino at all. They said it would bring more job opportunities for everybody because unemployment was so high. The people working here are from the reservation, except the managers. They say it will bring in money to our reservation, but I don't think it has.

At school, we're doing a project where we have to come up with ideas for bringing in money to the reservation and report it to our tribal council. A lot of students thought up different, exciting things that would help the reservation a lot. Me and a friend of mine came up with a movie theater, and some more of my friends came up with a restaurant. Someone said a swimming pool and a drug rehabilitation center. One wants to work on a riverboat that gives riverboat rides. I also think we could have a gas station, like an all-night 7-11, because people go for days without gas for their cars because we only have one gas station here and they don't supply very much gas. That could bring jobs and help out the reservation a lot. I'm happy with my reservation right now the way it is, but there are some things that need to be done. I hope they take some of our ideas seriously and try and do something with them.

> Conditions on many reservations are so poor they rival the most devastated inner cities. For example, on the Oglala Sioux Pine Ridge reservation in western South Dakota, the annual per capita income averages $2,000 and unemployment runs at 80 percent.

There are between 700 and 1000 people here on Lower Brule. I don't think people are doing well because a lot of them are still unemployed and they don't have nobody working in their family. There is a lot of people on aid and getting different help from the government, and I think that needs to be lowered a lot. People need to get out and work more. They need to earn their own money. People take advantage a lot. But it is kind of hard trying to find a job around here. I think some people are just trying to stay sober because there is a lot of alcohol around. As far as the quality of living here, it's not that good. It's home, but I want to make changes, too!

I would like to see us build things for young people my age because all we have right now is a teen center and a lot of kids are growing out of it. It's been up for about a year and a half. People don't go down there. They go somewhere else and drink, just to get away. They think, "Well, there's nothing to do around here except drink" because everybody else does. Adults go off the reservation and buy alcohol and bring it back here and sell it, so it somehow gets to minors. I think it would help a lot to build something more for people my age.

*A*lcohol is a major problem—is there a lot of peer pressure? There is a lot of peer pressure, but I can say no. It's hard because I'm related to everybody. Most of my relatives and my cousins, they all have done alcohol or drugs once or twice—or they do it all the time! My friends do it once in a while. I have to say no to them because I don't want to do it, but I'm scared I might hurt their feelings. Sometimes they just go along with it and I go out and I just watch them. If you want to, you do; if you don't, they'll leave you alone.

*O*n the reservation you have a tribal council. What does that do? The tribal council makes up our government, our laws, what we should do and shouldn't do. It is made up of the chairman, vice chairman, secretary, treasurer, and three council members. They vote on proposals, like whether to have a powwow on a certain day.

I try to get into our tribal government as much as I can. I think they are pretty effective. They are okay right now, but I just hope they'll help me in what I'm trying to do for my people in the future.

As far as the federal government, it should, if we make up rules, let us go by them. But if it's something they don't approve of, then they usually jump in. The Bureau of Indian Affairs provides us with money for our schools and funding for most of the projects we do. HUD [the Department of Housing and Urban Development] built most of the houses here.

*W*here have you learned about the federal government and the tribal government? Most of it I've learned in school, though I do learn about the federal government by watching the news. I also have learned a lot about the tribal government at home. Sometimes my mom and dad get into an argument because they both have relatives on the tribal council. My dad is our chairman's cousin, and my mom has an uncle and a cousin on the council.

ow would you describe an ideal citizen? Very supportive of anything that goes on in the community. They should be more concerned about kids and try to keep them from drinking and drugs and stuff like that. And taking care of our elders—everyone I know respects their elders. Making sure everything is okay.

o you think many people on the reservation fit your description of a good citizen? About 65 percent, I think. They are glad to be free. A lot of them fought in wars [for the United States], and I don't know why. They weren't even citizens until June 1924! The others probably couldn't care less. There are some that don't like to do nothing, that wish they could just get out of Lower Brule, that it's nothing but a hole in the ground. They aren't supportive of anything. They don't do much.

hich of the rights of being an American citizen do you value most? Freedom of speech. Because I think I should have a right to say what I feel and for somebody else to listen if they want to. I'd say also freedom of religion because that's our culture, that's what we'll always have and what should always be there for us. And we really value that freedom because the Native American religion was only recognized in 1978.

hat do you think is the biggest problem we face in the country right now? Abuse of drugs and alcohol and homelessness. When I was in Washington, D.C., it was hard to walk away from those people I'd see on the streets when they asked me for money. I'd usually give them some. They told us to be careful, though, because my teacher said one year she took some students up there and she gave somebody on the street some money and he went wild and said, "You have more than that, you can give me more than that!" He chased her. So, I'd give them my change and then hurry away. Homelessness is a big problem here, too.

*I*f you had the power to do something about those problems, what would you do? For the homeless, I would first try to build shelters and feed them. I know they have those now, but they don't have enough; isn't that the problem? So I'd just build more. And for the drugs and alcohol thing, I'd get them to go into rehabilitation to try and get them in the right direction.

*I*f you could change one thing about the way the U.S. government works, what would it be? I guess I wouldn't really change anything. I'm not really into politics.

*D*o you trust politicians? Not really. I don't know very much about them, but what I do know I don't trust them. What I don't like about tribal politics or politicians is that they are too confusing. I just don't understand it. Now that I've been to Washington twice, I'm starting to understand a little bit of it.

*W*ould you ever run for public office? Yeah, in my hometown. For the tribal council or something. After I get out of college, I could run for chairman—no, chairwoman! I just want to see some changes around here that would help a lot of the people. I'd probably want to come back and help the teenage kids, so they won't have to go through what I did. I would help them stay sober, have places to hang out and stuff. And I want to do things to keep the tribe going. People say this tribe is going to die out. That's what I'm scared of.

I don't believe that's going to happen, but I am getting frightened now because I'm almost out of high school and I'll be going to college. But I probably won't want to leave here for college because I'm scared there will be nothing left when I come back.

*W*hat do you think the country is going to be like in fifty years? I think everything will be a lot different from what it is now. I don't know if there will be tribes—but I hope there will be. There is going to be a lot more drugs. I think there will be a lot more drugs and a lot more crime. I don't really like to think about the future very much.

*D*o you think you've been well served by the U.S. government? Do you mean do I feel cheated out of anything? No.

*W*hat about in your history as a Native American? Well, I heard different stories from my grandparents and at the school. I just found out this year about Wounded Knee, which happened in 1892. I always thought it was a battle. I thought they were fighting back. And then my mom told me it wasn't a battle. It was a massacre. I guess one of the Indians got mouthy or something with one of those soldiers, so they lined them all up and just shot them—around 300 people in all.

Right now that's what I'm doing my research paper on. I'm trying to learn more about it. What I want to know is *why?* That is my question, that's what I'm trying to answer, why did they do that?

*W*hat did you think of the Presidential election last year? I only saw parts of it. I would have voted for Clinton. He'll do better; I know he will.

In the *S*uburbs

"Think for yourself."

Holly Lynn Haynes

Like many teens, Holly Haynes took a part-time job to earn extra money. After many weeks of passing trays, scrubbing dishes, and serving food at the local hospital four or five nights a week, Holly realized that work was interfering with school. But the family's need forced her to keep her job to pay for car insurance and clothes, and to save for college and medical school. Seventeen-year-old Holly lives with her mother and grandparents in a quiet middle-class Chicago suburb. Despite the hardships of the recession, the Haynes family continually opens its arms to those in need. Upon entering the house, visitors are warmly greeted by three dogs—once unwanted strays— who have been adopted and loved. Holly, herself a committed community supporter who plays the flute and loves to debate, has volunteered at the local hospital since the eighth grade. An independent thinker, Holly plans to graduate high school early to begin college.

Tell me how you got started volunteering. My mom encouraged me because she would see people on TV, like working in soup kitchens. She would say, "We really don't have money to do stuff, but we have all this spare time. We should volunteer." So she called up a nursing home—my mom always starts things for me [*laughing*]—and I went in. I would talk to patients and stuff like that. Later, I started volunteering at the hospital. I would work on surgical floors maybe, do little errands for the nurses, or maybe restock blood. And I would talk with the patients and help with feeding the patients if they couldn't feed themselves.

My most memorable volunteer experience was in the nursery, where I volunteered the most. What I did was rock the babies if they were crying, change them, feed them, bring them up to their mothers. When the doctors were there, I would help hold them or quiet them down. And I'm really glad that I did that because I got a lot of self-satisfaction out of it because I enjoy helping people. The reward is there when they smile back at you. It makes me feel so good about myself. Also I learn a lot from the doctors. That's the main thing that made me want to become a doctor. By volunteering, I also got my job at the hospital in food service.

How would you define volunteering? Volunteering at hospitals such as I did, or bringing food to make Thanksgiving baskets. Volunteering on Christmas Day at soup kitchens. Giving people food who wouldn't normally have a family to eat with. I think volunteering mainly is helping another person. A lot of people see volunteering as working in an office, and in a way that's helping a person to get their job done, but for me, I'd rather help a person who doesn't have what everyone else has or who maybe needs it more personally. I prefer direct patient contact or helping people in the community.

I think maybe that high schools should make volunteer work more available, more advertised, to the student body instead of requiring it, because if they made it look more appealing, more students would do it. In our school, I think I'm the only volunteer at the hospital—which is surprising because I know a lot of people at school who, if they knew about it, would want to do it. If there was someone in the guidance office that could call around to neighborhood hospitals, I think more people would be involved. Educate students more about what they can do, and how they can actually go about doing it.

As a doctor, I want to continue volunteering. You know you see all these commercials about Third World countries; once I'm established and everything I would like to volunteer some weeks out of every year over there, helping them in some way. Or even a poor place in America. Life is too precious. My mom has taught me to value it so much, that I hate to see it go to waste. Even if I can help in just the smallest way, that can make me happy.

The Haynes family dinner discussion ranged from whether to use "a" or "an" before words beginning with "h" to the crisis in Somalia. Holly's mother, Toni, summed up the family's outlook by saying:

> **Even though we've been affected here by the economy, I look at situations like that [in Somalia] and feel very fortunate. Can you imagine only eating boiled potatoes or nothing at all?**

So you think you can make a difference?
Yeah [*nodding*], I do. I'm not talking about like, I'm going to win a Nobel Prize or something, but just work within one community, a small community that nobody's heard of, or just one person's life. I could do something like that.

Do you think that Americans are willing to give their time and support their communities? There is an effort but maybe not as big as it should be. I think people care, but when push comes to shove, people think, "Either they eat or I eat comfortably"—and it's usually, "I eat comfortably."

If every person could just volunteer a couple of hours a week, that wouldn't be hard for them to do, and it would make more people's lives better. I think you get much more out of helping someone than by watching TV, and you take much more pride in doing so.

I don't want to deny that I do want to have money and I do care a lot about myself, but I personally also care about politics and the way the government is run because that's my future. But I see this all the time in school: kids are just like, they don't care, they don't pay attention, they never would watch TV to watch the news or anything like that. You ask them, "What do you want to do after college?"—they say, "Oh, I want to make a lot of money," or "I want to marry a rich guy." But I don't think I'm like that. I think those of us who care are the minority among high school students, but I think there are other people.

How has the recession affected you? How have you changed because of it?

A lot of ways. First of all, I don't think I necessarily started working because of the recession, but like this year I wanted to quit my job because it was interfering with school and my grades were starting to fall—and I realized that I couldn't just quit my job. My mother is an executive secretary, and she hasn't been getting raises. And my grandfather just retired last year, so another major source of income is gone from our family. We used to have the money to go to the movies when we wanted to. We didn't have to think about spending money; it was no big deal. My mother used to put away so much money every month into her savings, and she can't do that any more.

> More than five million kids between the ages of twelve and seventeen now work, according to the Simmons Market Research Bureau. In addition, a 1991 study showed that students who work twenty or more hours per week are more likely to experience a significant drop in their grade point averages.

So I can't quit my job. This is maybe a stupid example, but where I work, I have to wear nylons every day, and if I need nylons, I have to buy them myself because my mom just doesn't have the extra money. Or like lunch money or money for field trips and stuff. So it's important to keep that income, even though I was able to cut my hours.

In the past, I'd say, "Well, mom, I'm under eighteen; it's your responsibility to make sure I'm fed and stuff like that." [But lately] I figure she can't even buy things for herself. So I just took it more or less upon myself. I used to shop like nobody's business! [*Laughing*] Now I usually only buy things on sale, and I try not to even go shopping.

*Y*our father is not here. Does he help out? Does he know how you're struggling? I was born in Tennessee; that's where he and his family are from. My mom and dad were divorced when I was nine months old. And that's when I moved here. My father was ordered to pay a certain amount of child support every month. But the amount he pays today is the same amount that he paid when I was nine months old. They've never gone to court to change it. He never wants to pay his fair share. The only thing he was fair about was my braces. It just seems like we get so little money from him. Like I'm really into music, and I have a really top-of-the-line flute, a Yamaha, and it's like my prized possession—but he never helps out with that. The sad part of it is that he lives in Bellevue, Tennessee, right near Andrew Jackson's mansion, and he has a mansion himself. I don't talk to my father much. He's pretty much out of the picture—I think even for college.

*H*as the recession had an impact on this community? One thing that makes me mad is that a lot of kids at school think there is no recession. They have the attitude, well, vote for Bush again—it's good right now. And I think, yeah, you come from a two-income family, you have your mom and your dad, and you don't feel it like I do. To try to get them to see what you see is impossible. They just don't think like that. It upsets me. Especially when they say, "What's wrong? There is nothing wrong!" It's easy for them to say!

*S*o did the recession get you fired up about the presidential election? Yeah. I knew I did not want Bush in office again. I knew what was going on around me, even though I guess things started to improve right before the election. But still, I didn't trust him. And it wasn't necessarily that I thought that Clinton or Perot would be better, but I would have voted against Bush. A lot of the kids at school would say, "Well, I would vote for Bush," and I know they say that because that's what they hear at home. They don't form their own opinions. I didn't watch too much of the election, but I think I would have voted for Perot. I know that my mom voted for Clinton, but see, I wouldn't just have voted for Clinton because my mom did. A lot of the kids at school form their opinions that way, but I say: think for yourself!

*W*hat would be your idea of an ideal American citizen? Someone who's not perfect, you know, like the Cleavers [from "Leave It to Beaver"]. Everyone has their faults. But someone who respects the place that they live in, their town, their country, respects the people that they live with, regardless of their age, race, whatever it may be. Someone who volunteers their time, makes their own effort to do what they can, to take part. Someone who works, not lives off welfare. Someone who tries to work with others and doesn't have any prejudices against anyone else is what I would consider to be an [ideal] American citizen.

*D*o you think there's prejudice in American society? Oh, I do, and I can see where it's drawn from, very easily. I go to a school where, I don't know what percentage, but a lot of the school is Hispanic. I don't like to see myself as prejudiced, but every time I get bumped into, or threatened to get beaten up, or someone's just rude like screaming across your ear or talking back to the teacher or smoking in the bathroom, or doing something to a kid's personal property, the person is Hispanic. And I think that's where a lot of the prejudice is derived from.

The thing that kills me is in class they'll speak Spanish, like during class, about the class, not necessarily about socializing, and I'm like, "Wait a minute, this class is taught in English. I have to understand what you're saying in order to hear your opinion!" A lot of it is their culture, and a lot of times the guys are macho because their fathers are macho—and that goes for all guys, not just Hispanics in particular.

Now if I'd grown up with my father, I'm sure I would be prejudiced against blacks, because that's how they are, people who've grown up in the South. Once I was down there visiting—it was January, because normally I go there on my birthday—and a picture of Martin Luther King was on the calendar, and they said, like "what an ugly nigger," and talking like that, and I didn't know what to say.

Sometimes I wish it wasn't so. I almost make an effort to be friends [with] or to help people who are of a different race. I guess in some way I'm trying to prove that I'm not prejudiced. I'm trying hard because a lot of the people I know, my friends, are [prejudiced].

*D*oes being with people of different ethnic backgrounds affect your thinking? At school, I think most of the Hispanic students—I kind of stereotype them. Then, when I go to work and I have friends there that are black and Hispanic, they're so nice. They're the nicest people in the world; they're no different from anyone else. Well, see, this is why you can't have prejudice. A person is a person because of what's inside them, not because of their color.

I hear a lot of racial slurs at school. If we could just forget about that. . . . Maybe if we made them feel more important. I'm not saying that they're all in a slump, but I think it's important for everyone to have a high self-esteem. I have high self-esteem, and I wish everybody could be like that because they're missing a lot out of life by not loving themselves.

*H*ow would you describe yourself? Last year at this time, I thought I had the highest self-esteem of anyone that I knew. Then I applied for the National Honor Society at school. I'm third in my class, I had 350 volunteer hours, I had all these other leadership positions, first chair in band, and all this stuff. And I was rejected. So for a long time, I was just so depressed and my grades went down. I went from straight As to all Bs. And I began to think that maybe I am a brat, and I think I'm something good and I'm not. My self-esteem went so low.

When I was in junior high, I always used to say, "Do I look okay, does my hair look okay?" I was just always worried; then I never worried about it for the longest time; and now I'm starting to worry again—"Does my hair look okay?" Stupid insecurities that I have. I think a lot of it is caused by that big blow; it just totally caught me off guard. I think I learned—well, next time I'm rejected, it won't be as big of a thing. I've learned to deal with rejection more. I didn't want to! But I did. And I learned not to take everything so seriously.

*B*arely 50 percent of the voting age population votes on election day. How do you think voting is tied to citizenship? A lot of people say they don't vote because they don't make a difference. It's really the electoral college that elects the president. Well, I think the electoral college should have been gone a long time ago because it's just a formality. But I think every vote does count, whether you vote for who you want in, or you vote to have someone out, or you write "Mickey Mouse." By writing "Mickey Mouse" down, you're saying, "Well, this nation is crazy, who could put one of these men into office?" At least you're making your statement, and you're not just sitting back and saying, "I don't care." By not voting, you're not working with others to make America a better place to live in.

*W*hich right or freedom from the Bill of Rights would you never give up? I would say, basically, freedom of speech and freedom of the press. I can say or have published whatever I want. I can always state my opinion. Like in communist countries or whatever, you get shot if you go and talk about the president. I could tell Bill Clinton to his face that I thought he was a jerk, and they couldn't do anything to me. Not that I would do that. But also to read whatever I want. They banned a lot of books at one time; frankly, I don't see why. I mean, I know why, but I don't agree with the reason.

*W*hat is your opinion of politicians in the United States? Not very high. From what I've seen, I doubt that there are very many politicians who are honestly there to help the community—not out to make a buck or anything like that. But I think a lot of times we get such a bad opinion of politicians because of the media. I wonder what it would be like if there were no media, because they just play everything up. So sometimes you gotta get it on your own and figure it out. Like when they said Clinton was dodging the draft during Vietnam. Well, nobody wanted to fight in that war. I don't think it was such a bad thing on his part.

Because my opinion is formed by the media, it may not be fair to say that most politicians are dishonest. But from what I've seen, it seems like they are. Or maybe that they don't mean to be, but that's one of the chief things that the media plays up. You rarely hear of how good they are. I have respect for people who can tell us, point blank, what they're gonna do, and why they're doing it—instead of people who just are interested in winning and name-calling.

Would you ever go into politics yourself? You know, I've actually been thinking about it—which is scary for me. I love to debate with people. I'm a quick thinker when I'm debating. And I think I would represent what the people want to hear, what they want done, instead of just name-calling and everything. And I don't think I would go into it for money, 'cause I don't think there's a whole lot of money in it—it's more power, you know. You know I'm kind of a feminist—and I wouldn't be able to sit there with a weenie little guy as my opponent and have him just act like a big male chau-

vinist. I mean, I'd kill him! I couldn't keep control! [*Laughing*] But I think there should be more women in office. So I don't know—I'll have to see.

So you're a feminist, huh? Yeah, I am, a little bit. A lot of times my physics teacher will write out a test and he'll say, "The scientist did this and this, and what did *he* mean?" and I'll cross it out and put "she" and circle it. My American history teacher will always say, "We need your dad's signature," and I say, "What about my mom's signature?" I don't think he does it on purpose. But stuff like that.

My mom works her butt off at this company. Then, she got her degree, but she's still a secretary. She could do so much more. Women don't have close to equal opportunity. Sometimes I think it may be the same for a white woman and a black man—in terms of equal opportunity. I really think if the government were in the hands of women, that instead of wars, there might be a checkers game or something. I know this is way off beat—but I think why can't we just compromise? If it were just a competition, no one would be killed. I hope someday women do get equal opportunity.

When I was like four or five, I used to get *Highlights* magazine, and my mom would read it to me. In one of them, there was a question: who is smarter in math, boys or girls? And the answer was boys. And I cried and cried. I'd say, "Mom, I want to be smart in math!" Now I pay attention, and I try to catch when guys are being chauvinist and I'll correct them or something. I wish it could be different.

My doctor is a woman. When she was in medical school, she was the only woman. They used to harass her, and she would just get back at them. I'm sure there's going to be that when I go through school, but I'm not going to tolerate any of it. I'm not afraid to slap someone. Let 'em sue me, I don't care. I just won't be walked over.

Do you think the government is doing a good job? Well, I don't know. Right now, I don't think they're doing terrible—I am not on the street in rags. But I think they could be doing better to make the middle-class family, like ours, live more comfortably, and not have to live from paycheck to paycheck. And get us out of this recession. But I think basically, overall, they're doing a good job. But then again, I don't know what to compare. Like what's an excellent job? I've only understood actually what's going on for maybe three or four years in government. Before, I was naive to it. I didn't realize what everything meant and how important it was.

What do you think President Clinton should do to help middle-class families like yours? Well, I don't think he should be taxing us. But I think he should raise taxes. I liked Ross Perot's idea of putting 50 cents tax on a gallon of gas; that's a lot of money but if you did it for a few years, it could work. It could bring us out of this recession. It would be very hard for me to pay that, but I think it's better than taxing millions of dollars on middle-class families who don't have the money.

I hate to see them take money away from education too because that is what I will have to do this year—apply for financial aid. I would like to see them take more money away from the military. I'm not big on war at all. I mean, I'm not like a peace child or anything, but I think . . . wasn't it Reagan who took all the money and put it into war, like Star Wars? I think that may have been a waste. I think it's necessary to keep up with other countries, to a point, but why surpass them? This is part of the reason I wish I were more educated in political science, so I could advise and write letters.

One thing the government spends money on is welfare. What do you think of the welfare system? Let me tell you what I think is bad first. A lot of unemployed people will take welfare because it pays more than a job at McDonald's. Again, I think it all ties in with doing your part as a citizen, where you don't live off of our money to do nothing. I think you should work for your keep, whether you work at McDonald's to get started or whatever. I think maybe welfare should be a little bit more . . . I don't know if "strict" is the right word, but I think they should investigate because there are people who live off welfare that shouldn't be. If they work at McDonald's and still don't have enough money, then maybe they can receive a little bit of the welfare to help them get on their feet. But I think welfare is a good idea because there are people who just can't afford to live, and I think it's bad in that people can afford to live off of it.

What direction do you think the country's going in? Right now, I think it's just kind of here. It's not going up; it's not really going down. Here's what I would like to see: I would like to see more women in office, more women running things. I would like to see less politics and red tape involved; I would like to see politicians making a difference, more than just enjoying the power that they have. I would also like to see people better educated, because I think our country is falling behind in education. We need a stronger education system to educate these people, so that when they are in government or wherever they are, they know what to do. I think a lot of times we're pampered in school, but once you get out in the real world, nobody is going to pamper you.

***W**hat do you think is the foremost problem facing the country?* I think the biggest problem facing America is the people who don't have homes, the people who are living on their own. A lot of people don't vote because they have more important things to do, like finding a meal, finding a place to spend the night. If we help them, maybe volunteer to build houses or whatever, to get them on their feet, then in turn they can help America to get on its feet. Then we'll have more people to fight other problems. Once we have our own problems taken care of, we can help the poor and homeless in other countries.

***H**ave you heard the term "American dream"? What does it mean to you?*
The American dream to me is that you grow up, showing respect for each other but receiving the same respect. I think mostly it's to work for myself, to do what I want to do, and not to have to settle for a job like I have now for the rest of my life. Of course, I want to get married and have children and everything. I don't want to be like super-rich; I want to live comfortably. But I think the American dream to me is just getting through all that and being able to do it and say, "Look what I've achieved, and this is how I did it." Show it to younger people and be a role model for them. Also, I always want to keep volunteering.

"Just do the right thing."

GERARDO GUERRO GED.

How many Americans know what it's like to want to order a hot dog at a fast-food restaurant and not know how to ask for it? Gerardo Guerra knows, as do many new immigrants struggling to adjust to a new language and a new country. He came to the United States from Tampico, Mexico, in 1991 as an A student ready for college. But to master the language eighteen-year-old Gerardo went back to high school, and now lives in Baytown, Texas, with his parents and uncle. Studying hard, he tries to use new vocabulary at every chance, weathering the occasional public embarrassment that comes with speaking a foreign language. Gerardo enjoys many aspects of American life, like fast freeways, Chinese food, and music. He experiences many of America's problems such as racism and discrimination as his family struggles to make ends meet. Yet he feels his chances of success are better here than they were in the poverty of Mexico.

*W*hat were your first impressions of America? I didn't know how to communicate with the other people. Just "hi" and "table" and "thank you" and a few words. Everybody was speaking English, the person who was beside me, behind me, everybody. And I couldn't understand it. That was my first impression. I was scared. I thought, "What am I going to do? I don't understand it!" I can remember the first time I went to the store, and I wanted to buy a hot dog. I don't know how to call it. So I was pointing.

So when I wanted to go to the store to buy something, I would have to go with other people who knew English so they could translate. And I remember the first day at school. I couldn't find my rooms. I didn't know the numbers in English either. Like the room 321, I didn't know how to say it. The only thing I could do was show a person the number, and then she understood what I meant. Then, she showed me the way to my room. It is very hard to communicate without any knowledge of English. It is hard.

Sometimes when my teacher told me something, I understood another thing. And then the teacher asked me, "What are you doing?" And [*with exasperation*] I answered, "Well, you told me to do this!" And the teacher says, "No, I didn't. I told you this and this."

I think if a person comes here to the United States, the first thing that they have to know is English because you have to be able to communicate with the other people.

*D*o you think that public signs should be in English and Spanish? No. [*Shaking head firmly*] I completely agree that you have to learn English. I don't like the idea of two languages on signs.

Most people come here to get a job. To get a better life than they could have in the other country. So, if you want to get a good job, you have to learn English, you have to know it. There is no way around it. It is the only way.

*D*o you think it's easy to get a job once you learn English? Yes, it is very easy. You can go and apply at any store. If they select you, all right. You can do the job if you are able to communicate with your boss and the other people. That is very important.

I think that if you are prepared and get a better education, you are going to get a better job. You are going to make a sacrifice, study now. Afterwards, you are going to get the rewards.

I am so happy with this government. I am a student, and the government helps the students. The government provides to the students the opportunity to go to a high school. If you don't have a car, they provide the bus. They provide the books. Whatever you need.

In Mexico, you have to buy the books. And if you don't have the books, then you have to get with a friend and do the homework together. Here, you can take the classes you want. In Mexico, you can't do that—you have this class and this class and this class. In Mexico, the people who are rich—they can get jobs. Here, if you are able to do the work, you can get a job.

> " I think it's great, the efforts to educate new Americans. When I went to school, there were separate schools for Mexicans, separate schools for whites, separate schools for blacks. Now what they are doing is great. "
>
> Albert Contreras, Gerardo's uncle

In Mexico, I finished high school and was ready to go to college. But my sister asked me, "You want to come here, to the United States?" And I told her no. And she said, "Come on, try it, and then if you want to go back to Mexico, go." And I told her, "Okay, let's try it." And I'm here.

I would like to stay in the United States. I believe it's a kind country. The government offers to you the opportunity to get a job. That is why I like it.

*W*here did you get your ideas about America? I have seen by my own experiences, watching the news, reading the newspaper, and those things.

***W**hat do you think of the U.S. policy toward immigrants?* There is a lot of people who run illegally to this country. They come because they want to have a better way of living. But not all of the people who come love the country. And that is the problem. The government doesn't want the people running [illegally]. And the government is right. Because the government sees the people, the gangs, the Hispanic people, and those immigrants are doing nothing to help the community. There are good and bad people.

***D**id anyone ever try to get you to join a gang?* No, I don't have friends with the gangs. I don't go out with those people. They think they can do everything and they feel good making another person sad. They feel good destroying things. They feel some power.

According to the Latino National Political Survey, the majority of Hispanics in America speak English as their main language, love the United States, and do not favor increased immigration.

***A**re you trying to keep Mexican customs?* Yeah, I like my customs. The food, tostadas. There is a lot of Mexican things that I like, and there is a lot of American food that I like, like pizza. Is pizza American food? I love pizza. One thing, I won't forget my customs, because I lived in Mexico seventeen years, and I have my customs inside me.

***W**hat do you like doing in America?* I play the drums at the church. I want to learn how to play the guitar. Sometimes I take the guitar and start to practice something. And another thing that I do is I go to church, and at the church, there are computers. I like the computers. So I work on them. Those are the things that I do when I have free time.

Did I tell you that I work? I do. It is not work like formal work. I work in a house just one day or two days a week. I clean this woman's pool, the cars, that's it. I don't call it a job. I don't earn

very much. It is better than nothing. The money that I earn, I spend maybe when I want to go buy some clothes or I save it.

I like computers and want a computer career. I studied electronics in Mexico. I know how to fix TVs and radios. I know how to change the parts. I like to take out everything from the radio and see what happens. But I have never opened a computer, and I would like to know how to use it, how it works, what they have inside.

***W**hat's your definition of an American?* The people who live in the United States, the people who take care of the country. The people who are working to improve the country, to get a better country. Americans are born here. They have to have papers that say you are Mexican or American.

***Y**ou're not a citizen yet, but would you vote if you could?* Yeah, if I could, yeah! In my opinion, my opinion is valid, like [President] Bush's opinion, like Mrs. Peña's [his teacher's] opinion, like everybody's opinions. They are equal. And they together make a decision for a country or for a community.

It's important that everybody vote. Everybody counts. If I could vote, I would do it. The people who don't vote, they won't agree with the decision. The government will have problems. If you don't vote, you don't have the right to talk, you didn't participate, you don't have the right to say.

If there are a thousand people thinking that their vote doesn't matter, and they change and vote, it may change the election. And if they vote, and all of the people vote, it is going to be clearer—the actual majority is going to elect the president.

Is there one right you think you would never give up? Freedom of expression. The freedom to speak. You can say your point of view. I think it would be the most important.

In Mexico, there is the right to speak—but you say your opinion and the government does what they want. You vote, they count the votes—then they put the president they want in power. Mexico's president is Carlos Salinas de Gortari. I think another person was elected, but the government put him in power. And the people said, "Why is this man elected?" There is freedom of speaking, but the government does what they want. The government doesn't care what your opinion is.

Would you run for political office? Yeah! I would do that. Because I would represent the Hispanic people. It is important, because in some places, Hispanic people have a low image. How can I explain? Okay, there is an American here, and there is a Hispanic here. Both are applying for a job. The boss will interview them. Even if they are equal, sometimes the boss gives the job to the American. What happened with the Hispanic?

I would like to be a congressman or something like that to represent the Hispanic people and to give the Hispanic people a better image. There are a lot of bad Hispanic people, but there are a lot of good Hispanic people.

Is the white community open to the Hispanic community? No! How can I tell you? If you go to the white community, and you are Hispanic or black or from another country, you can be black, and pay for a house, and the house is yours. But your neighbors and the people who work in the stores—some of them are not friendly, and they make you feel not very good. But not all of them are like that.

In Mexico, we are all Mexicans. All the people eat with all of the people. There is no problem.

But here, Hispanic people eat with the Hispanic people, the black people eat with the black people, the white people are with the white people—everywhere. That is what I don't like. I have seen some blacks, they don't like the Mexicans, and I have seen some Mexicans who don't like whites, and whites who don't like both Mexicans and blacks. [*Laughs*] Everybody are brothers and sisters. They don't have to separate.

What do you think could bring people together? I think that wiping out racism, taking out that. It will be better for the blacks, whites, and Hispanics. Providing institutions. Giving to [people of different races] education and understanding. Giving the opportunities to everybody to vote, giving the same things to everybody.

Do you think that the government is doing a good job? I don't know. I don't know much about the president [George Bush]. I have heard commentaries about him. Some are good, some are bad. But maybe he does a good job. I am not sure. Like everything, there are bad things and good things. Nobody's perfect. So that depends on the point of view.

Well, I like one thing that he did. He opened the free trade agreement with Mexico. I think that is a good thing.

I think it is going to help Mexico. The people that live in Mexico, they don't have jobs, and I think it is going to open more jobs. From their point of view, it is going to help the Mexicans, the people.

*D*o you think it is good for the United States too? Yeah, because they are going to build factories there, and they are going to take from Mexico natural resources. Mexico has a lot of natural resources. They are going to work there and take out the oil, whatever, wherever the factory is. I think it is going to be good for the Americans too. I think that is why Bush accepted it.

*W*hat would you change about American government? I don't know a lot about the government. One thing that I don't like is corruption. There are some bad policemen. Not all the policeman, just a few. I just watched the news, and they killed a black man. Sometimes they are racist, you know—discrimination. They think that they can do whatever they want because they have a gun right there.

If I could change the government, I would clear all of the police, all of the corruption, and take care of dirty dealers. They have to serve the community and take care of the community. They don't have the right to kill another person. Nobody has the right to kill anybody; only God can do that.

And I would open more opportunities for the Hispanics, like an English school, or a school where they teach English a little more and for free, because the numbers of Hispanics are increasing. Every day there are more Hispanics and more people coming from other countries, like maybe from Europe. I would open opportunities for them, like the opportunity to get a job, without discrimination.

*W*hat do you think America will be like in the future? Is it going in the right direction? That depends who the president is. That is a hard question. I think that it's going to be good if the government keeps the same ideas that they have and the same purpose to help the community and to help the country. It will be good.

*D*o you think Americans care about their country? No, not all. I think it is half and half. There are a lot of young people that don't care about school, that don't care about community.

*W*hat should each American do to be a good citizen? There are a lot of good Americans. Just do the right thing. If you have a job where you have influence over other people—then making the right decision, doing things to help other people. Take care of your job, your family, your community. Vote. Love your country. If your country needs something, then provide it.

If every community is taking care of itself, then we are going to have a safe country. We need to work together, have meetings, discuss how to help people [such as those] who don't speak English or any problem that could be in the community.

Right now, I work and study. After school, I want a career and to be a good professional. And then, I am going to help my community. I want to bring recognition and attention to my community and give my attention to the community.

I try to help. My church is in the middle of Old Baytown, where many of those Mexicans are vandals. One of the things they [church members] do is go speak to them and sometimes give them invitations for the musical group where I play the drums. We walk out, and we sing outside, and we show movies, and a couple of things.

We are doing it for our community to take out vandalism and violence. The community is helping us too. Because I speak to the people who do vandalism, and I try to convince him which way he should live his life. Then, he speaks to another person, and then the other person speaks to someone. It is a cycle. And it is helping. There are a lot of ways to help the community. This is the way I can help.

***W**hat do you think is special about America? What is the best part about living here?* Work and the opportunities. Because the United States has the doors open to job opportunities, to have better jobs. They have a free enterprise system. You can do whatever you want. Buy whatever you want. That is important. The special thing in this country that I like is that you have more opportunities than most places.

"Nothing good comes without sacrifice."

Rhett Rampton

From his letter sweater to his love of superheroes as a child, seventeen-year-old Rhett Rampton would fit in well on the "Andy Griffith Show" or "Father Knows Best." Rhett's beliefs are also firmly rooted in traditional values, most of which he credits to his church, the Church of Jesus Christ of Latter-Day Saints, whose members are also called Mormons. Rhett lives with his parents, two brothers, and one sister in Layton, Utah, not far from the heart of Mormon culture, Salt Lake City. He believes there are clear rights and wrongs in conduct and that the entertainment culture has blurred those lines to the detriment of society. He is now looking forward to his biggest adventure so far—a two-year mission on behalf of the church to teach scripture and convert people to Mormonism. Rhett looks forward to the challenge with his trademark attitude: good things come out of sacrifice and hard work.

*W*hat has it been like growing up here? Here in Layton, I had a really good childhood in a safe home environment. I've heard stories from other kids, and I think I'm lucky. My mom's home a lot, so that was good. As a child, I really liked superheroes. I liked to play Cowboys and Indians, stuff like that. And I remember when I was little, thinking how much fun it was going to be to go to high school.

And I am having a blast. I like the games, I like dating—I wish I went out more, though! [*Laughing*] I like the dances, just everything about it. I like to be involved.

The students here are mostly Caucasian, but there are some minorities and stuff. The main religion here is LDS [Latter-Day Saints], or Mormon. There are different groups, or cliques, like the cowboys. They don't really live on farms or anything like that, but I think they probably want to be cowboys. They just wear the boots and the Wranglers.

Then you have your mods; they dye their hair black and paint their faces white. You have your jocks and cheerleaders, that kind of group, and preppies—probably a lot like the other high schools have.

I can kind of go with any group, but I would like them to think of me as a really-fun-but-still-kind-of-preppy-type. School-oriented, smart, but not geeky, just kind of fun.

I also hope I give the impression as being reliable. I think it is important to have lots of friends. I like saying "hi" to people in the halls and people saying "hi" to me. It makes me feel good. And I hope I am a good friend to them.

I like to be like a mover and a shaker and be involved and know what is going on all the time. Right now, I am a PSA [Parent-Student Association] representative. I had to write up an application and go in for an interview. I am glad I did it; it has been so much fun. The parents here are really cool. Also, I like hobnobbing with the mayor and stuff. People say that's a good position for me just because I am more mature than some people. I like that.

*W*hat is a typical day like for you? There is not really such a thing. I usually plan to get to school a quarter after six or so in the morning.

Some of that is to maybe do a little reading or a little studying, but I have to admit a lot of that is kind of social, too. And then I have all of my classes. After school, I sometimes have meetings, cross-country practice, and now I'm rehearsing for the school musical, *The Mikado*. Fridays we have games and sometimes we have dances. So I'm away from home a lot.

It is fun, though I miss my family and stuff. Lately, I get up before they do and I get home after they have gone to sleep. They probably don't even know who I am any more. [*Laughing*]

*W*hat is the Mormon religion like? LDS is a Christian religion. Christ was in Jerusalem, but then when he was resurrected, we believe he came over here. Our religion is based on the Book of Mormon, which is about people who were in the Americas when Christ came here. Together with the Bible, it is a full set of scripture. There is a thing called Articles of Faith, and it is just twelve sentences that explain everything our church believes in.

We have the president of the church—we call him the prophet—then there are two counselors and there are twelve apostles and the general authorities and leaders of the church. We don't have a preacher, either; we have a bishop. It is expected of young men who are worthy to go on missions. Usually it is after you are nineteen. You go and concentrate on missionary work, teaching people the Gospel and trying to convert them. So after high school and maybe a few months of college, I will probably go for two years. You go wherever you are called. There are a lot of missions in other countries, but there are some in the United States, too.

I am looking forward to it, but I can wait. I am having so much fun in high school right now. Some guys might have a problem with it, being a little scared, but I am excited. Some people say it is two years out of your life, but I think: what could be more important than doing the Lord's work for two years?

The Church also advocates scouting. I just earned my Eagle Scout badge. I definitely agree with the purposes and values of Boy Scouts, like being a good citizen and following the oath.

Usually once a week in church, we have had what is called a Mutual. That is for boys and girls who are twelve to eighteen to get together for an activity. Usually it is a pretty fun thing related to the Gospel. At church every Sunday we have what is called a Sacrameeting where the bread and water are taken.

I take a church-sponsored seminary class. I get out of school and I just walk across the parking lot to another building. It's kind of like a Sunday school. You learn scripture history and sometimes memorize scripture that might help you when you are on a mission. It tries to help you to be a better person. It is kinda like church during the week. Most of the students here attend. That is probably one of the best classes here.

> We believe in being honest, true, chaste, benevolent, virtuous and in doing good to all men; indeed, we may say that we follow the admonition of Paul— We believe all things, we hope all things, we have endured many things, and hope to be able to endure all things. If there is anything virtuous, lovely or of good report or praiseworthy, we seek after these things.
>
> From the Articles of Faith of the Church of Jesus Christ of Latter-Day Saints, by Joseph Smith.

A lot of people sometimes might say Utah is too strict because of the church—that it stinks. But it doesn't. I have an article from *Business Week* magazine, and it had a whole bunch of stuff on Utah. As far as health care, we have one of the best systems in the nation; in education, we have the highest number of high school graduates in the country. We have the least teenage pregnancies and dropouts. If you look at this, it's pretty good compared to the rest of the nation.

I think it is probably better here than a lot of other places. It is safe here. We don't believe in drinking or smoking or any of that. We don't drink caffeine drinks either, such as tea or coffee. The church is strongly opposed to teenage sex, so I see little of that problem around here. We have *a lot* less problems than other schools, I think. Sometimes if I turn on the TV and see all of this stuff about what is happening in high schools and stuff, I am really glad I live here.

But I also think, where is America going? From the Book of Mormon, we believe it's a prophecy that this country would be the strongest country in the world if only the people would keep the commandments of God. But somewhere in Minnesota, they don't even say the pledge of allegiance! We say that in all of our assemblies.

What is this? [*Shaking head*] I get tired of all this . . . not to bark at the ACLU or anything—but religion is what this country is founded on! It seems like people keep saying church and state, church and state, church and state. Before, they always used to have prayers in public meetings. I was talking to my brother and he said if you look at papers or notes that Madison took at the Constitutional Convention, he would go over to a tavern, eat there and stuff—he probably had something to drink, too—but anyway he would write what it was like in the convention and in there, it says that they felt divine guidance! I even heard lately that they are trying to take the part in history books about coming here for religious purposes out, and instead just say that they came here for freedom. I don't know why—because it might influence someone's mind? [*Sarcastically*]

I get mad at stuff like that! I have pride in my school. I have pride in my hometown, and my state, and my country, and it just hurts me to see stuff like this and I just think, why are we doing all of this stuff?

*W*hat is it about the ACLU that you disagree with? They have probably done some good things, I'm sure. But some of the things, like prayers in schools or government meetings—especially in government—that is probably where you need divine guidance the most! I do not see why they want to take it out. And, personally, if someone was of another sect or religion or something, and offered a prayer that was maybe not exactly the way I would pray, but if it was sincere, I would still think that God would hear that. Maybe we could have a moment of silence where everybody could just pray to their own God, so to speak.

Look how much worse things have gotten now that they have started to take these things away—drugs and alcohol, divorced parents, teenage pregnancies, crime. I was looking at these charts in a magazine showing how much crime there was before 1962, when they really started getting big on school prayer and things like that, and then it showed how much there had been after that. And the difference was like this! [*Arms spread wide apart*]

I just do not understand why they say school prayer is not constitutional. Look at the Declaration of Independence. I think it talks about divine guidance or mentions God several times in there. In Washington's farewell address, he said something about if this nation would stay close to God, it would be better. They never print that in textbooks any more. They never printed the story about when he was in the French and Indian War, everybody was trying to shoot him, and when the battle was over, he had like four bullet holes in his coat, two horses had been shot out from under him, and he had gunpowder in his hair. And he said that he felt he had been saved by divine power. And you never hear stories like that anymore, because it might "influence somebody"—maybe to do good [*sarcastically*], I don't know. Religion is a big part of my life, so it kind of goes with everything. Certain things like that scare me because it is getting closer and closer to maybe suppressing religion. Sometimes it scares me, all of this liberal stuff.

*H*ow has being in LDS affected your outlook on life? After high school I would like to get a job till I go on my mission. I have no idea exactly what, but, to me, I feel like I am a big boy now and I want to take care of myself. A lot of families help pay for their son's missionary, because it is expensive, like $350 a month to live and eat. But I want to support myself or pay for most of it. So I will probably work and then go to school. Then I'll go on the mission. After I come home, I would go back to school. Then hopefully, a little while after that, I would like to get married in the temple. We believe that if you get married in the temple, then you are married for all eternity if you stay worthy throughout the rest of your mortal life. So that is the big thing right there, and that is about as far as my plans go.

I would like to have lots of kids. A lot of families around here do have lots of kids, like seven, eight, nine. LDS encourages you to have children. The church is for families—they encourage taking one day out of the week to do what is called Family Home Meeting where you just do something with your family. It is mainly so you can be with your family and learn "family values." [*Sarcastically*]

*W*hy do you say it like that? Just because [President] Bush got made fun of so bad for that. I kind of agree with what he is saying, but the way that they did it—like the Murphy Brown thing—they did come across a little stupid. I question TV anymore, though. As soon as I turn it on, I turn it off because of the things that are discussed on it, like being promiscuous and teenagers losing their virginity. You see so many people who are single and pregnant. I realize that there are occasions for divorce and everything. But I understood what [Bush] meant. I feel bad for families sometimes because of the things that are discussed on TV.

It's kind of like the saying, "If you want to smell like manure, hang around it." I think it's better to surround yourself with good people because they will build you up, and the same with good books and good movies. But if you go and see trashy movies, it just brings you down and it does probably make you imitate what you see.

*H*ow do you think the country is doing overall? I think it's going down. Going back to the scripture a little bit, it says that if you don't keep the commandments, then the nation will fall. That kind of scares me because maybe that is part of the reason why we are having all these economic problems.

*D*o you see any way to change that? Start by not being so liberal. I am a positive person, I don't think we're all going down tomorrow or anything like that, and I know we are a lot better than the other countries. We just need to quit falling and start climbing back up again.

Change would be a joint effort, because I know the president cannot really do anything if the people will not follow it. So it could come from the bottom up. But there does need to be some leadership in government to do that.

*W*hat did you think of the presidential election? I didn't like it. Clinton is too liberal. I do not think Clinton is exactly the best person for the job. He campaigned really hard, I have to give him that. I think he is kind of slick though and he made way too many promises. Another thing I do not like about him was the way he went about representing America in his cabinet. People talk about racial and gender equality, but it works both ways, too. There are jobs out there where they have to hire so many minorities that it might take away from a white Caucasian who might be more qualified. And the same things with colleges.

If you hire or appoint a woman to the Cabinet just because she is a woman . . . I don't know if I like that. If she is the best person for the job, then, yes, she should get it. I just think that those people who work harder or who are the best should get the reward.

As far as gender, I do not know if this is right or not, but it seems like women have lost respect because they are trying to be equal. Like the kinds of movies I have seen lately compared to a lot of the older movies—it seemed in the older ones they treat women differently and they have more respect and won't say certain things in front of them. But now movies are different. It makes you wonder.

People probably think I am a little goofy, but I kind of liked Perot. He has a lot of charisma. I remember him saying that if the main problem with America is economic, then why not hire a person who is knowledgeable in the economy, a business person, to get us out of it? And correct me if I am wrong, but I thought that during one of the debates that Perot was the person that talked about the gas tax, and everybody thought, "Oh, he is stupid." And isn't Clinton doing that now? But "Oh, how wonderful!" [*Mockingly*] Though, if raising taxes is going to help our country, then, yes, we should do it. If it does help us out of debt, then we need to do whatever it is to get out of it. Nothing good comes without sacrifice.

*W*hat characteristics would your ideal president have? First of all, he would need to have intelligence; that is the big key. He also can't be a pansy. He has to be tough, and I would like a president who would say what he really thinks when he is campaigning. That is another thing I did not like about Clinton: it seemed like he was for everything. I think a good president would say, "No, I am not going to do that." He should be honest and definitely a hard worker. He must care about what happens, and maybe not so much about elections. He has to have some guts—it is important to be advised and to have advisers, but not to let them push you the way they want something to happen.

> " Overall, we're a conservative community here, though we differ on things, like any community does. Many people here wanted Perot [for president]. I think the next generation really sees the problems we face—though some, I think, are afraid to face them. "
>
> Jan Rawlins,
> student body advisor

I really liked Washington. Everybody liked him, of course, and from what I read, he was the ultimate leader. I liked Lincoln also. If you look at pictures, you can see how much they aged because of what was happening in their term of presidency. They kind of gave their life for their country. [*Pause, thinking*] When I was little, I liked superheroes and that superhero personage—truth, justice, and the American way.

*W*hat do you think are your responsibilities as an American? Obeying the laws, voting, being informed and educated, educating your children. A lot of it goes back to education, and I think we need more of an education about government, because sometimes people talk about "This is wrong in the country," but they don't really have any real solutions. That even includes me sometimes on many questions, because I have not studied it yet.

So where have you learned most of what you know at this point? I have a lot of my family in this area. We get together sometimes, and sometimes after we eat, the guys kind of go off and talk politics or law. So I used to like to go sit and listen to what they talk about. Then a lot of it is just from talking to other students and reading. Just articles, like in the dentist office, something like that—articles that I pick up around school.

Which one of your rights as a citizen do you value the most? It is hard to say, because they kind of go hand in hand. The right to the pursuit of happiness and freedom of religion. Freedom to congregate in groups, form organizations, assemblies. Those are probably the ones that are the most basic—they ensure other rights. Those are the things that I depend on. Freedom of religion: that is a big part of my life.

Do you trust politicians? Some. I think they kind of have a bad name, but I think there are some that are trustworthy. I met the mayor of Clinton [Utah]; he is a good guy. I thought he was going to be stiff, but he wasn't. He's funny and really nice. I think some are really good, but there are others that aren't.

What do you think about Congress? We have what is called a Roundtable at school, and that is where representatives from every class come together to made decisions on certain policies or things for our constitution. This is just high school, but I kind of see how hard it is to get things passed and things moving. In Congress, though, I also think a lot of that is due to a lack of leadership and discipline. If they just do what is right, then things would go a lot better and faster. I get a little bit tired of party things, too. Because of the two factions, they can't work. If they just knock it off, things would go a lot smoother.

*S*ince you have a little bit of experience in student government, could you ever see yourself running for a political office? I would always want to be involved, maybe on committees and stuff, maybe small town politics. But I do not know if I would really like to make a career out of it. Maybe if you were doing it to get ahead, you wouldn't always make the right decisions.

*W*hat do you think is the biggest problem facing the country right now? It all kind of goes to morals, because if people had morals, then you wouldn't have crime, prisons, and police. And hate and racial things. If everybody is in harmony with everything, then the economy would go better. I think TV is a good thing if it is used right. It is a marvelous invention. But too many people just sit there and vegetate, and then they start believing things they see. I don't know if you have ever read *1984* but it was talking about where people would no longer be able to think for themselves. Apparently that is what TV is doing.

People say you're not supposed to teach about values stuff at school, but you should. Wrong is wrong and right is right. So occasionally, that form of education could be better. Have you ever watched a "Leave It to Beaver" or those other shows? Have you ever seen one when they are in school? The teachers have control; there is discipline. And they teach kids rules. It needs to be a little bit more of that. There are still basic things that are wrong, like lying and a lot of stuff like that.

*D*o you think that one person can make a difference? There is a story— I hope I get it right. In the Civil War, I think it was General Sheridan, he was twenty miles away from his troops when they were attacked. When he finally got word, he rode back. When he got there, his men were frantic and some of them had started to run. And I remember he rode up and down his lines yelling, "I am here, I am here. Turn around. We will win this battle." And just because he was there, his men felt safe and trusted in his leadership and they won the battle. That actually happened. I think one person can make a difference.

*W**ho are your heroes?*** My parents, probably. Just because of the way they are and present themselves. I always see my dad reading. They continually try to better themselves. I also admire my grandfather on my mom's side. When he was younger, his mother had died and the rest of the family farmed the kids out to relatives or neighbors, but he stayed with his dad and his older brother. When he was about thirteen, he decided that there was not a whole lot for him there. He did not run away from them or anything, but he struck out on his own and he has been on the go since then. I think that is neat. That is why it is important for me to pay for things myself. Maybe that is where it comes from.

When I was younger, I used to admire Robert E. Lee just because of his style and his charisma and people felt they could trust him and his leadership. He is still highly revered in the North as well as the South. He was just a gentleman and a leader. I admire former church leaders whose biographies I have read. I like Superman. [*Smiling*] It is that same thing about one person can make a difference. Standing for all that's right. Always trying to do your best.

*H**ow would you describe yourself?*** [*Rolls eyes*] Reliable, good. Always wants to do right, does not want to hurt anybody—but if they do something wrong, then justice needs to be served. I hope people see me as a good friend and loyal, hardworking.

*J**f you could pick any country in the world to live in, including the United States, which one would you choose?*** The United States. I really like the American dream and it impresses me—people who start from the bottom and work all the way to the top. I admire people who do that. It's probably also just the freedoms and opportunities that are here— achieving anything you want, which comes through education and a lot of hard work and determination.

For me, I don't want to be a Donald Trump or anyone like that. I just want to be happy. That's all. I need to make some money, but what I really need is family and friends—that is where, for me, all happiness derives from.

"Stop and listen and think."

Caine Pelzer

In a place where street kids are pulled back from the edge of a troubled life, Caine Pelzer has learned to control his anger, respect his peers, and study hard in school. At fourteen, Caine is still a young boy, but his distanced gaze and reserved manner betray some harsh realities of inner-city life. He grew up in Brooklyn and the Bronx, many of his friends belonged to gangs and posses, and his older brother went to jail for stealing jackets. Then Caine's father died, leaving eleven-year-old Caine as the oldest man in the house, with more responsibility—and anger. Truancy and "not listenin'" finally landed him at New York's Edwin Gould Academy, a residential school in the suburbs for students deemed at-risk of dropping out. Caine has learned that gunfire and drugs are not necessarily the norm, and to enjoy simple alternatives to fighting, such as playing basketball, drawing, and falling asleep to jazz music.

*T**ell me about where you grew up.* I grew up in Brooklyn. I got one big brother and two little brothers, and four sisters. At first I was living around Crown Heights. Then, when I was six, my house burned down on Glenmore Avenue, so we went to a hotel—but weren't paying for nothing. Then they sent us to a shelter in Brooklyn. We stayed there for about four years. The shelter didn't make me feel homeless, but it made me feel close to homeless 'cause it wasn't really a house and we were just staying there because the state provided it.

It was a good place. They had block parties and stuff, and a church. They had an afterschool program that I enjoyed going to. But my family wasn't doing good. I was part of the problem because my mom would have to go up to the school [when I got in trouble] when she could have been at work, making money so we could move out of the shelter. I was doing most of the bad stuff, and I didn't stay in the shelter that much. I shouldn't have been doing that.

Then my mother got a job in the Bronx when I was ten, so we moved up there. My father was still with us. Later, he was in the hospital. They said he kept bleeding and stuff. He went into a coma for about a month. Then, when I was thirteen, he just passed away—he never came out of the coma. He had cancer.

At first, it was a little bit shaky. It was hard to do our regular routine, because we were used to having our father there. And my older brother was locked up for three years for stealing coats and stuff. I had to look after my little brothers, and help my mother out with the shopping. When she was at work overtime, I had to go shopping by myself and keep the house in order.

*W**hen did you first start getting into trouble?* When I moved to Amroy, my brothers and I got to know everybody around. Then, my brothers—they were eleven and thirteen then—began fighting out there and I started fighting with them. They called me the bad boy around the block because I used to fight people whenever I wanted to.

*W**hy did you like fighting?* 'Cause I found people I could beat.

If I were just a kid, smaller than you, walking down the street, what would cause you to pick a fight with me? Say you was riding your bike, and I didn't have my bike, and I said, "Let me get a ride." And you tried to run from me. When I catch you, I'm gonna fight you because you ran from me.

So you would yank me off my bike and punch me? Um-hmm.

If I were crying, you wouldn't feel bad? I'd feel bad, but I wouldn't give you the bike back at the time. I wouldn't steal it, but I'd ride it around the park and I'd lay it down next to you when I was done.

Why did you feel that you had a right to do that? Because I hadn't met my match. When I did meet my match—that's when I stopped. That day, we were playing basketball, and this kid threw the ball at my brother. My brother didn't want to fight him, so everybody said, "Oh, Caine, you're gonna let him hit your brother and not do nothing?" So, I went up to him, and we started fighting and he threw me against the gate. Then I said, "Hold it right there—don't touch my mouth—alright? I'm gonna catch you later." I don't like getting hit in my face.

I stopped beating on the smaller kids too. Because if I beat on them, then they are going to get somebody who could beat on me. So that was when I basically stopped and I started using my head.

But I also started cutting school there. My mother didn't really find out about what I was doing until I told her that I had to stay home, but she said, "No way." And then I told her that I had been skipping school for over one year.

What did your mom do when she found out you were skipping that much? Gave me a whipping! After that I started going to school, until I moved out to the Bronx, where I met some more friends and started cutting school again.

I skipped school for half the year and they still graduated me from the school. I knew everything. The school told my mother, "He is a bright kid; he just won't come to school." So they passed me and I went on to the seventh grade and I got kicked out of that school in the Bronx, for cutting and stuff. You remember where that kid got stabbed last year? That was my school.

One day, a guy told me [residential school] was a place where you have fun and stuff. I was like, "Oh yeah? I want to go there. How do I get there—be bad? I can do that." So I did. I wasn't listening to my mom. I wasn't disrespecting her or cursing or nothing. But if she told me to go to school, I wouldn't listen. If she told me to help my brothers, I wouldn't. If she told me to do my homework, I didn't know how to do it. She was like, "Why don't you know how to do it?" Then, I said, "I missed this." And she said, "You want to know why you missed it? Because you cutting school—playing hookey."

One day, my mother said, "Come on, we're going to my job." And I said, "Your job's not this way." We were on the train, and we went to the family court. I said, "What am I doing here?" And she said, "You're going to go where you say you want to go." And they sent me upstate to a place called Little Flower. I was there for about a year.

The staff was very strict. Every time I didn't do my homework, they made me write "I will do my homework" about three hundred times on paper. And I thought, "Oh, this is hard." So after I did that for a year, I was telling my mother that I wanted to come home and that I was straightening up—had got my act together. That was it. I went home. Then I just started messing up again.

I would go out to go to school in the morning, and I got on the bus. Then on the way to school, I would see my friends walking the opposite way. So I would just get off the bus and go with them.

*W**as it the school or your friends that made you skip?** It wasn't school. It was probably that I wanted to be down and stuff. I wanted to stay with the group—not by myself all the time. That's it.

*W**hat does it mean to be "down"?** Say I went to a party. And I had permission from my mother to go, but you didn't. And you went anyway. You want to be down—you want to be with your friends instead of doing what you're supposed to do.

*W**ere a lot of kids doing things that they weren't supposed to do?** Yeah. Because they wasn't disciplined. At night, we will be walking around, and it will be eight o'clock, and I say, "Yo, I gotta go home now." And they be like, "Why you going home now? I'm going home at twelve o'clock in the morning!" And I'll be like, "Oh, yeah? Well, I'll go home at three o'clock in the morning!" We'll just be going back and forth. And I will stay out that late, even though I had my head set to go home at eight o'clock, when my mom wanted me to come eat dinner. I wasn't listening to my mom; I was listening to my friends.

*W**as it worth it?** Nope! I would rather just listen to my mother instead of listening to my friends now. When I go home now [from Edwin Gould], all the friends that I used to cut school with look at me like, "Oh, where you goin'?" I said, "I'm going to school because I've got everything set up now." My sister tells my friends, "Don't get mad—'cause he doing the right thing and you guys are out here doing the wrong thing."

How have they helped you here at Edwin Gould? They helped me learn how to hold my anger—if somebody wants to aggravate me, I know how to not get frustrated. I know how to think positively and not let other people take from me. You can't find too many schools like this in the city—people that really want you to learn.

Before my father passed away, he told me, "You got to stop cutting school because you ain't going to hurt nobody but yourself. One day, I am not going to be here, you better listen now, while I'm here." And I was like, "Alright."

So when he passed away, I was feeling guilty because I hadn't listened to him and stuff. I had put stress on the family, you know. That is when I really stopped. It changed my future.

I stopped lying. I was straight up with my mother. I started treating my mother better and trying to get the trust back from my family.

That's it. I am going to school all the time now.

> **Here we teach them that it's okay to have problems. Then we teach them that they have to learn to deal with them, and we teach them how to do that.**
>
> Gary Payne, a team leader at Edwin Gould Academy

Were you in a gang? I wasn't in a gang, but I used to run around with them. They used to ride around on the back of buses. One day I rode on the back of the bus with them. I was scared that I was going to get caught. And at the back of the bus is a black rail, and it could fall off any time if there is too much weight on it. With the vibration of the bus, I was thinking that it wasn't secure and able to hold all these people. And I was so scared that I jumped off while the bus was moving on the highway, but the cars stopped behind me. And that was last time I was with those kids in Brooklyn.

*D*id you think that what the gang members were doing was wrong? Yeah, but I just wanted to be down. So I went along with them, but I never beat on an old lady or nothing. I just went along on the bus ride. But then I was figuring in my head, "Oh, they ain't my friends!" Because when I fell off the bus, they were laughing at me.

*W*hat is a posse? Say you got like thirteen people who want to hang together. They go and do stuff, like going on the highways where it's dark and beat people up and take their money. That's what posses usually do. You can't find that many posses that do positive things, like help people out in the supermarket or somethin'. You don't find too many people doing that in the city.

If I wanted to be in a posse, I would have to go and beat somebody up real bad or try to kill him or something. You got to show them that you ain't scared to do stuff, and that you aren't scared to beat, hurt, and rob people. You ain't scared of the cops—if the cops came up to you, you wouldn't cry—but you would stand up there and curse in their faces. They name themselves after cartoons, like "The Transformers," and stuff like that. They just run around and start stuff.

Gangs don't usually beat up on people; they usually hang out at parties. If some of them don't have enough money to go to the party, they are going to rob an old lady—they won't beat up on her—they just snatch her purse and run or something. But a posse, they would beat the old lady and let her sit there and cry, with her head bleeding or something—and they won't even take the purse. If one person out of twelve people takes the purse, and the cops catch him, then he will get in more trouble than the rest. That's why they usually don't take stuff. They will just beat on her, just to have fun.

I've also heard that gangs and posses ride the subways in New York. Is that true? Yeah. Say I was on a train, and I had a coat that was pure leather with goose inside of it. And they were saying, "Hey, yo, give me your coat." And I say, "No," then they would beat me and take the coat just for the coat. If you get caught up with a gang on the train, there is no way of getting out of it, 'cause if you give up the coat, they are still going to beat on you so you don't have enough time to run and get the cops. And if you don't want to give up the coat, and you fight them back, you are gonna get beat up anyway.

When I go home and ride the train, I stay in the middle, where the conductor is—his door is usually open. So if somebody comes in there and they touch me, I will go and stand by the conductor. If they want to get me, the conductor will put me inside the door and close it.

I saw one good movie—*Alive*—the story of a plane crash and people that had to survive in the snow. And there was nobody fighting one another. Instead they learned how to survive off one another. They wasn't killing nobody; they was saving themselves. It was cannibalism, but the people who died gave the others the okay to eat them after they died. They didn't try to kill one another and weren't fighting. But for a posse, on the streets, if they had to survive and say they only had one chicken, they would fight each other for that chicken, and when they were done fighting, nothing would be left. The posses, they don't look out for one another like the people in this movie did.

***W**hat do you think is the biggest problem facing the country and what could President Clinton do about it?* [*Long pause*] Fighting one another. We just keep fighting one another—we don't think about the real stuff that could be happening. [Clinton could] learn how to handle all of it. Learn how to take matters into his own hands. Because right now, he is one of the main people that can do stuff like that, as the president. He can bring more cops in to stop things right as problems are starting, not while they're about to end—because that is going to cause more [trouble], and it will keep spreading. If they know how to just nip it in the bud, then everything will be straight around here.

***W**hat direction do you see the country heading—uphill or downhill?* I think it's going downhill. We have all these people with AIDS—they don't help—they are just waiting for a cure, they don't want to do nothing with their life, they are just making each other pregnant—all they basically want to do is spread AIDS. That's the way I look at it. If you are waiting for a cure, then you have got to wait patiently, and not just give everybody AIDS. That's why I think we're going downhill because if everybody really wanted to stop the AIDS virus, they would stop passing it along.

*A*nyone ever try to get you to deal drugs? Yeah. A couple of people. One person, he actually said, "If you sell drugs for me, the cops will never catch you, 'cause I got two 'nines [nine millimeter pistols]. If the cops ever chase you, just run up to my house, lock the door, and shoot 'em." I was like, "I'll do that." But my brother yanked me, and said, "You better not sell no drugs—if I catch you selling drugs, I'll try to beat you up." So I didn't.

I also came close to doing it once when my friend went like this [*holding out his arm as if to give something away*]. The cops were searching people, and he said, "Caine, hey, take this up to my house." So I said, "No, I ain't taking it." And I threw it on the floor and the cops grabbed it. And they asked, "Whose is this?" They checked me, I didn't have nothing on me, and they checked the other person, and he did. They took him away. One kid that I knew was killed—shot for selling drugs.

My family talked me out of [doing and dealing drugs]. They tried to teach me right from wrong. People do drugs to make them feel good. If you go up to a drug dealer who is just starting out, and you say, "Hey, yo, you ever kill somebody in your life?" And they'll be like, "No." And I say, "So why you selling drugs? When you giving people crack, that is killing them." They don't look at stuff like that, they just look at killing is only "bam," you shoot 'em and he's dead.

*D*o you trust the police? Yeah, I trust the police. But while I was around my friends, they used to be like, "I hate the cops." But I say, "Then when somebody trying to kill you, you'll like the cops, right?" They'll be like, "Naw, we'll always hate the cops." If you act right to the cops, they'll act right to you. If you want to be Mr. Tough Guy, then they will show you a rough time.

*W*hat did you think of Ice-T's song "Cop Killer"? Songs like that, like Ice-T and Ice Cube are doing, about the killing of cops and cops killing people, that's hyping people up. Ice-T says that he's a rapper and he ain't doing nothing wrong, but he is making people in the city want to go kill cops, and he's making cops angry about the songs, and the cops are wanting to hurt people. By him making that song, it's just mixing everything up. And he ain't doing nothing but making the money off of that song.

*D*o you think that government affects your life in any way? No, not really.

*H*ow would you like to see government affect your life? Probably helping other people. And they don't really help other people that much. I am talking about helping people with their drug problem, like bringing more cops into the system. If they doing that, they are helping me, 'cause that is on my mind.

*W*hat do you think can be done to help communities like the Bronx? Everybody just working as one. People in the cities need to stop trying to kill one another. If everybody was trying to work as one, there wouldn't be all this drug dealing. If everybody was trying to do the right thing, we wouldn't have as many diseases around, such as AIDS.

The most I could probably do is talk to them and try to encourage them to stop. That's probably it. Because the only way you can help somebody, if they don't see the light, is to make sure that somebody else that is close to them sees the light, and that person can maybe help them out.

*H*ave others ever looked to you as a role model? Yeah. My little brothers. When I was younger, I used to tell my brother, "Now, you go ahead to school." He would say, "But, Caine, you cut school, so why can't I do it?" So I would say, "We're two different people." But one day, I did take him and we cut school together. I thought he was right behind me, but he got on one train and I got on another. I tried to follow him, but he didn't get off the train. So I went home, and my mother asked, "Where is your brother?" and I told her, "He's coming," but I didn't know if he knew how to get home. She said, "Well, sorry, but don't you come back without him." So I went outside looking around for him. Then, when I went back to the house, he was already there. My mother asked, "Why did you take him with you?" And I was like, "He asked me to." So she said, "If he asked if he could jump off the roof, would you let him?" I was like, "No, 'cause that's my little brother!" And she came back with, "Well, why did you take him today?" I was scared that day because I thought something had happened to him.

Now, whatever I do, like if I want to go to a slumber party, he wants to come. So I take him, because he's my little brother—it's something positive we can do. When I go home, I do good things, like buying games and stuff that he would like. Now, I'm showing my brother the right way, and anything that I'm doing is positive, and he is fol-lowing everything that I'm doing.

When I help him, he is going to help somebody else, and the person that he helps is going to help another. It is just going down the line.

I also had a summer youth job with the athletic league. I basically helped with everything, like taking the kids to the park. The kids were around six years old, and we played around and gave them their snack. We had to look after the kids while on trips. It was to show them how to have a good time the right way.

The kids really listened to me; they didn't give me no hard time at all. I didn't scream at them or nothing. I talked to them in a nice tone and told them what they had to do. If they say, "We'll play," I would say, "Yeah, you're gonna play if you *listen*—if you don't listen, you're not gonna play." So they basically listened to what I said.

*W*ho are your heroes? Arnold Schwarzenegger and Leroy Smith, a bodybuilder. They not only got the strength, they use their heads. If you can use both, you can get around in life. If someone is trying to hurt you, and you know how to use your power, then you can avoid getting hurt.

*D*o you trust politicians? I believe them at the time [during the campaign]. But some people will say stuff just to get in on it. Then, when they get in, they just go the opposite of what they say. Like Bush said, "No new taxes." But once he got in, he changed that.

*W*hat do you think are qualifications to be a leader? To show people that you have enough strength, and that you don't give up easily, and that you are doing everything that you can to succeed.

*T*eenagers are often criticized for not knowing or caring about what is going on. What do you think about that? The other people out there, they don't think that people care, but I care, and I want somebody to care about what I care about. So I listen to other people, and would like them to listen to what I think.

I think the kids care, but they don't want to show that they really care. The people that say "I don't care" are the ones that are being bad, and people don't usually see people who act bad show their true colors.

*H*ow do you know what you know about government? Because my mother, when I go home, always talks to me about it. She tells me about national news, like how Clinton is going to make change. And he should, since he is the leader of the United States, and even the world. He is doing a good job so far, so I am going to try to follow him all the way.

*D*o you think your parents were good parents? Yeah. They show me what's right and wrong. When she punishes me, my mom tells me, "Caine, I'm not doing this to hurt you, I'm doing it to help you." And

I realize that, because I'm learning from my mistakes now. She just knows how to handle herself—unlike people in the city, they always get outta hand and they want to fight. She always says that there is a way to avoid it. She is a good teacher.

What kind of parent do you think you'll be? I'm going to be the same as my father and I won't lie to nobody; I'll be straight up with them. I'll treat them with the utmost respect.

What is your idea of a good citizen? I haven't really thought about that. Well, do what they are supposed to do, such as getting an education. If everybody had an education, this world would probably be a better place, and everybody would be doing the right thing, instead of the wrong thing. People should like school as much as they like their hobby. People should be listening and learning knowledge from one another. They need to stop and listen and think about the things they do.

What do you think is the most important right that you have as an American? Being free to do what I want to do. Get an education. Have a good life.

Do you think that you have any responsibilities as an American? Yeah. I got responsibilities like taking care of myself, looking out for others. Treat my family with the utmost respect. Staying out of trouble, doing the right thing. If I am looking out for my family, and if they are doing good stuff, that will make the community better.

Do you think that people have different rights and responsibilities in other countries? Some places I've heard they have slaves or prisoners wanting to get out. I don't know where it's at, but there are some places where they have less privileges and rights than we do.

***W**hat experiences have you had with discrimination?* One kid called me a *moreno,* and I didn't know what that meant in Spanish. When I asked him, he said [*in a degrading manner*], a black person. He said, "I don't want that *moreno* playing with me." I just left.

Then, I felt that if he was black, he wouldn't want to be talked to like that. So I usually say, "Would you want that done to you?"

I don't think that it's getting any better. If I, being black, went up to a Puerto Rican [selling drugs], and I said, "Yo, let me work for you," he'll let me work for him. But if I was to get caught by the cops, he wouldn't try to get me out of jail. If a Puerto Rican man got locked up by the cops, he would try to get him out.

If you're black, there is no need for you to sell drugs, because you have got more abilities to do whatever you want to do. And [Puerto Rican drug dealers] must have less abilities, because they only sell drugs and don't want to do the right thing. So don't sell drugs for them. If you want to do something, get a [legitimate] organization of your own, and make something of yourself.

***D**o you think you can do that—make something of yourself?* Yeah. [*Nodding confidently*]

***W**hat would you like to do?* Be a technician or a mechanic. Because I'm good with tools and stuff. I'm good at fixing bikes. Like if you gave me the parts of a bike, I'll put the bike together with no problem. When I get more experience, it will be easy for me to put a car together, so it will be a good job for me.

***W**hy did you want to do the interview?* Because my teachers said that they would be proud of me, and that it was something positive that I could do. Mr. Donlevy told me that it would be a good experience, and I thought it would too. So if I were interviewed in a job or anything, I would know how to act—and I think I would be more calm.

***W**as it a good experience?* Yeah.

"I have to live two days in a day."

Cindy Marie Gibson

"I'm scared." Seventeen-year-old Cindy Gibson is frank about her fears. She has AIDS, contracted through a life-saving blood transfusion that she needed to stop complications from sickle-cell anemia, a disease she's had since birth. At first, Cindy and her family tried to hide her illness from their small-town community of Brunswick, Maryland, because they didn't want her to be ostracized like Ryan White or Ricky Ray. But being locked in the solitary confinement of keeping her secret to herself was hurting Cindy so much that she decided to risk telling everyone. She wrote a moving letter to her peers, and though she expected to be shunned, she was greeted with nothing less than open arms. That boost and the support of her family has helped renew Cindy's determination to get the most out of her life, whether it be short or long. She's witty and loves a good laugh, but is serious about helping others understand that what people with AIDS really need is friendship.

***W**hen did you find out that you were HIV-positive?* My parents found out in '85. I was almost ten years old. But I wasn't told until two years later. My first words were, "Oh my God! Am I gonna die?" which is usual for anybody when they find out something like that. I found out I had full-blown AIDS last summer.

When I found out I had AIDS, I was mad. If I had a punching bag, I would have probably torn it to pieces. I was sitting in a chair and I was with my psychologist and my dad and mom, and I told them that I hated them. I sat in that chair and stomped my feet, hit the chair, I did everything I could to that chair. Then after I calmed down, I apologized to my parents, and I let them know that I was mad at them because they didn't tell me when they first found out.

At the time, I was in the middle of getting a job. I tutored at the middle school two days a week in reading, spelling, language arts, and math. One of my best friends in eleventh grade worked there, too. She was talking about her boyfriend, and I was talking about mine. I showed her his picture and she was like, "Oh, he's cute!" I told her I was afraid I was going to lose him, and she said, "Why?" and I go, "Well, I have to tell him something he might not like." She was like, "What?" She was my best friend and I knew she could keep a secret, so I told her. She was the first one who knew outside of my family. She supported me. But then she went back up to the school office and—you know how you write and you talk out loud when you get into your writing? Well, she was writing a letter to me saying that I shouldn't think that I'm going to lose her as a friend, and she was like, "I can't believe Cindy has HIV." And the lady who got me the job walked through the office and said, "Are you sure Cindy has HIV?" The next thing I know I'm at my therapist's office, and my mom says, "Cindy, I got a phone call earlier" from the lady who got me the job. And she goes, "And she wanted to make sure that all she heard was correct." I was really mad and I did it again—I hit the chair.

***W**hy were you trying to keep it a secret?* Because me and Mom and Dad were in the process of working it out to get it out in public, but we wanted to do it smoothly. We had a meeting with a few teachers that were going to teach me this whole year to let them know that

"Cindy has AIDS, and you have the choice if you want to be her teacher or not. If you don't, that's fine; we hold no bad feelings against you." Those teachers said, "Fine, we don't care, we'll teach her, she's a great person." We were trying to make it smooth.

I also felt real bad because I had just started dating this guy and I already knew I had to tell him that I had HIV. Then when they told me I had to tell him I had AIDS, that was even worse.

But I never got to tell him because we broke up. I think he knew before we broke up because my mom called his mom to let her know what we needed to tell him. He broke up with me, saying that we go to two different schools which are pretty far away. I still believe that he knew before we broke up and that's why he broke up with me. And that was really hard. It hurts, because I really need that companionship, but I don't know if I'll ever get it. I'm hoping, but I don't know.

> An estimated 1 million Americans carry the HIV virus that causes AIDS; about 30,000 Americans died of AIDS in 1992.

A guy can't get stuff out of me that he can get out of other girls. And I don't want a guy to go out with me because he pities me. I just want a guy because I need that friendship, that relationship. I could never give a guy exactly what he wants. It doesn't matter if I practice safe sex or what; nothing is 100 percent safe. Some guys think that [*macho voice*] sex is sex, you've got to have sex! But you don't have to. I know people think it's stupid, but cuddling is all some people need. That's all I really want. I want somebody who is close to me, and when I need it, a little companionship. That would be a great relationship. I want somebody to love me for me and not just to have a physical attraction. So far, that's not working, though.

*H*ow were you doing up until the time that you went public with this? I was doing okay, I guess. There was tension in the family. Mom and Dad would come home from work, and we would all yell at each other. We wouldn't do it on purpose. It was just we had so much anger inside of us, that was the only way to get it out. We couldn't hit each other—we wouldn't do that—but if we had a punching bag we would have used it. It hurt. It would get to the point where I would go in my room, slam the door. My parents would go in their room, slam the door. I heard them talking by themselves and I know they were crying a lot and I know it was hard. We were all having trouble with it. That's when we decided to go out with it because we just couldn't handle it any more. We went public with it, and we got a lot of support.

I had to go public before they could send a letter to the students of the school because it was against the rules of the board of education or something like that. I had the letter posted. It was in the newspaper and everybody at school read the newspaper. I was scared that day when I went to school, but I went anyway.

I was nervous because I didn't know how they would take it. I sort of expected them to shun me. Brunswick—I mean we're just a small town. We all try to stick to our own business. I don't know if it was because of the things I read about Ryan White or what. I just didn't trust the community to say, "Oh, we support you, don't worry." When I got off the school bus, I felt really stupid because I had thought the wrong things. I was surrounded by my cousin, one of my best friends, and other friends.

*W*hat has changed since the letter? I'm a lot more sociable. I try to do a lot more stuff. I like to go to the mall and bowling and stuff like that. I'm in a youth group at our church, and we do a lot. The first Sunday of every month we have a meeting, and then we clean this community center for money. Then we can go on trips. I try to stay well enough to do all that stuff. Last January we had a retreat planned, but I had pneumonia. I got out of the hospital a day before the trip. My dad and mom were like, "We don't want you to go," but I let them know that if they didn't let me go I was going to be depressed and bummed the rest of the week! They were so scared, "Oh, she is going to get sick, I know she is." But they let me go. I had a blast.

Overall, my parents say I'm more happy, more peaceful. I think I'm free. That's the best way to describe it. I'm free of this burden that I

used to have. It's a burden having AIDS, but it was more of a burden keeping it a secret. I am still a little bit quiet, but if you go to
school with me one day, you can tell I'm a little bit happier and I'm
not like I used to be because I act up in class now. I used to be in
special ed classes because if you have a disability or you're sick,
you could get in special ed classes so that you can have extra time
to do the work. I decided to go back to regular
classes after I went public. But out of a
whole year of classes, I miss approxi-
mately three months. Between sickle
cell and HIV and then finding out I had
AIDS, it has been pretty bad. But now
I've got the support of the whole
school, and if I need help, somebody
will try to help me. If I'm home from
school for a while, they'll call me, try
to visit me and stuff like that. It's
pretty cool.

> **The main thing is to know that no one can get this by just being a friend or little things like hugging, crying, or laughing with me. So don't be afraid to be a friend to me, I really need your friendship.**
>
> an excerpt from Cindy Gibson's letter to her peers at Brunswick High School in December 1992

My uncle tells me that I'm a lot more
mature than most kids my age. He
said that I have the mental capacity to be
older than I actually am because he said,
"Cindy, I think the AIDS does that to you." I
have to put my life in perspective—I could be alive three or four
years from now. I could be alive eighty years from now, but I have
to get my life all together.

But I'm a big goofball! [*Laughter*] I love to be a kid! I love to do
things that little kids love to do. Put me in a room with infants and
preschoolers, and I will have the time of my life. I'm serious! When
I'm in the hospital, I go in the playroom and talk to the babies, and
the babies laugh. I run around the halls with the two-year-olds.
They run around the hall screaming; I run right behind them
screaming. I can't have my own kids, but when I do grow up, when
I'm married—if I am—and all that, I'm going to adopt because I love
kids. They are innocent—sometimes.

A baby that is born with AIDS didn't ask for the AIDS. I'm not going
to have kids because number one, it might get sickle-cell anemia,

and number two, it will end up with AIDS. No baby deserves to be born with that. I didn't deserve to get it, Ryan White didn't deserve to get it, we didn't do anything to get it. We needed a blood transfusion to save our lives, so we took it.

Our parents didn't think, "Oh God, they might get AIDS from this." All they thought was, "This will give my baby life." So nobody asks for this. I certainly didn't ask for the sickle-cell anemia either, but that was the way I was born. I got it from my parents—they never knew that they even had the trait of sickle-cell. My brother lucked out. My mom and dad say that I got it because I was special. [*Smiling*] They do that to tease my brother.

*W*hat do you think people need to know about people who have AIDS? People are getting to know that you can't get it just by touching or by hugging. People need to know that we have feelings too. I'm not gay. That this isn't just a "gay" disease. It's everybody's disease. Innocent little babies get born with it sometimes, or the mother breastfeeds them and gives it to them that way. Everybody can get this disease. I've even found out cats can get it.

All the people who have AIDS want is when we're at home, alone, sick, and we can't make it out to work or to school, we need some-body to call us or come visit. When I get older and I move out of my parents' house and I get sick to where I can't go to school for a while, I'd like my friends to come over and maybe help me out with my house or my apartment. Or just come visit and talk to me, keep me up to date on what's going on in school or who is pregnant now or whatever [*giggles*], but I mean, that's how it is. We all want that friendship.

*D*o you think the government is doing enough to help? I believe in President Clinton. I think he is actually going to try his best, and I know it's going to be one heck of a disease to kill or to even try to help people that have it. He is going to give all the money he can. He'll try his darnedest to find more people who want to help people with AIDS. I think that the president is doing a good job, trying his best, and I think the country is going to turn around to where there are going to be a lot of people fighting this disease. Not just fighting it because they have it, but fighting it because they want to get rid of it for other people who have it. Just so that there isn't any disease like this for anybody.

Nobody knows that much about AIDS except that it's a hard disease to fight. I know they are trying to find ways to stop it so it doesn't progress, like with the drug AZT. I don't think the government can do more than what they are trying to do right now. They just need to keep up the research, and make donations to places where they are doing research or to places where they give out the money to people who have AIDS.

Are there any ways that government services have helped you? I'm not for sure. I know my mother has insurance, and that pays for most of the stuff. Right when we went public with it, my pastor called me and told me they were ready to lend me money any time we need it. We haven't taken advantage of that, but I know there will come a time that we will need it. My mom and dad hate to take money from people, even if they really want to give it to us. A man who read about me in the newspaper called and wanted to give us money. He said it would pretty much be "mad money," so I could buy whatever I want. He left a message on the answering machine saying that he wanted to send a sizeable check, and my mom got tears in her eyes. She was like, "Oh my goodness, we can't let him do that." But the man kept insisting. So my mom said okay.

What was it like to be on "Good Morning, America"? It was nice, but I was only on from 8:17 to like 8:30; I wasn't on there for long. A lot of my friends said they didn't do a very good job. I felt they did a great job considering they got me up there to New York. I've never stayed in a hotel in my life, and that was the best hotel I ever stayed in. [*Grinning*]

I went with my mom. We flew on a commuter flight, which was pretty cool because there were like five people on the plane. But I had gotten sick that weekend. I had a cough and I was very tired.

I was scared, too. I was supposed to be interviewed by Joan Lunden but she was in Florida doing a parade. The other person was really cool. We had like forty-five seconds to talk and she said, "All you've got to do is calm down and don't be nervous, just talk like you normally talk, answer the questions, and we'll be okay." And then she was like, "Good morning, it's 8:17 and we're here talking to. . . ." I was like, "Oh my God!" I was so scared. I was trying to not look at the lights, and I tried to keep focusing on the TV where I could see myself. I was trying to make sure I wasn't being stupid and acting nervous. I'm like, "If this is live, I'm in trouble." And it was. I was like, "God, if I mess up, everybody in Brunswick will be laughing at me!"

After it was all over and everything, Charles Gibson came over, and it was so funny because he goes, "Hello, cousin!" and shook my hand, and I looked at him and said, "You know, I always thought we were related, and I wasn't for sure till I met you." And we got our pictures taken with the whole crew. I enjoyed it. Before we went to "Good Morning, America," Fox 45 did me on the ten o'clock news. My aunt was teasing my mom; she goes, "If you get on Oprah, I'm going!"

That was my first trip to New York, so I wanted to go sightseeing after the show and they said sure, but we had to walk. So we walked from the hotel to Macy's because I wanted to see the Santa Claus. After Macy's, we went out to the Empire State Building. When we finally got to it, I was out of breath. We decided to go back to the hotel and went to bed!

How do you feel about all this attention? I like it. I think the more attention I get, the more all this stuff will get out. I can talk about AIDS, and I can tell people that it's something nobody wants. I don't know all the facts about AIDS, but the Frederick County Health Department has asked me to be in a group to go and speak at different high schools. And I think that is so cool! Before I went public with this, a woman there went to Frederick High to speak, and there were a few students who waited afterwards to talk to her and asked, "When are you going to bring us somebody who actually is our age who has AIDS and can talk to us about this?" Now, I'm ready emotionally to go out and help. I don't know how to speak about the stuff that well, but I can try my best—just speak from my experiences. I don't want people going out and having unprotected sex or people who have AIDS or HIV taking it out on other people.

*H*ow does having AIDS change your perspective on life? I have to live two days in a day. I do, because you never know when I could go. I could be here for three more years; I could be here for eighty or ninety more years. Hey, I could be 112 when I die! I'm gonna try to outlive my brother—he said he is gonna live till he's 105. So, I said, "Okay, I'll live till I'm 106!"

My brother is funny. He goofs off and he picks on me. He says he picks on me to make me strong. I think it does. I always scream at him, but it helps. It would help even more if he were here, but with him being at sea, I can't do much about that. He's in the Navy. He'll be going to the Persian Gulf. He said he should be back by November. I hope so; I can't wait to see him. I miss him.

*W*ho are your heroes? My parents, mainly. With me just going through adolescence, they went through a lot! Then, going through the problems with AIDS, sickle cell, and going into the hospital almost every month, they went through a lot to keep me alive. All the time I stay in the hospital, the one person who stays with me is my mom. I know it's hard for her because those cots aren't worth anything. She stays with me there, gets up in the morning and goes to work, and then comes back and stays with me again the next night. She does that no matter how long I stay.

I also think both sets of my grandparents are my heroes. My grandfather, my mom's dad, has black lung and he literally doesn't have a lung. My other grandfather, my dad's father, has cancer and he has fought it for five years and is still alive. They have got so much courage. I can't see how they do it. My dad's father doesn't talk about his pain. When we go down to visit him in West Virginia, I can tell he's sick, I can tell he hurts, but he doesn't talk about it. He'll ask me how I'm doing. I'm like, "I'm okay, tired, but okay." I'll say, "How are you feeling?" He'll say, "I'm fine, Cindy, ain't got a care in the world."

My grandmothers are great. I can tell you both sets of my grandparents spoil me. When we lived out in West Virginia, my dad's parents lived right across the street from us. I'd be over there every day. They'd have candy, and they'd say, "Cindy, there's a bag of chips, you want some?" And they still do it to me. I love them both. They just show so much courage. I don't know where I got my courage from, but if I'd say so, I got it from both sets of grandparents. It's hard because they are so far away and I miss them and I want to be there if anything happens. I don't want them to be lonely when they die.

What do you think about health care issues? I don't pay that much attention to the government except when it comes to stuff about the Navy because my brother is in it. But I know that they are having a lot of problems with health care and I think it's in bad shape right now. There are people out there who are poor and they have AIDS or they're just sick and maybe homeless and can't pay the bills. There should be like free clinics with enough resources for them.

How do you think the government is doing in general? I don't know that much. But I think they're doing okay. I can't say they are doing an excellent job, but they are trying. They've got the deficit. If they don't fix that now it's going to be here forever, and it's going to be even harder to pay four years down the road.

Do you trust politicians? Not really. [*Laughing*] If you look at it, the reason for the debt is because all those congressmen bounced checks. That's stupid. When a regular person bounces a check, they get in trouble, and when the politicians bounce a check, no big deal. That stinks. They get off easy, I think.

Do you know who your representative and senators are? I don't think so. I do know my mayor, though. I know the mayor and the council members. When I went public with my having AIDS, the mayor said, "We support you, and the community of Brunswick supports you."

*W*ould you ever run for political office yourself? No. I'm not a good leader. I just don't have the voice, the heart, to actually do that. A lot of people in politics hurt a lot of people who have helped them. I'm too sentimental. I don't think I could handle it because to get to the top you've got to step on a lot of people.

I need that support, and once you get to the top it all goes away. When all this happened and I went public and I got all these interviews and stuff, I tried to keep my feet on the ground although I kept going up into the clouds. I can't forget the people who helped me get through all this.

*W*hat did you think of the presidential election? It was a good race. I think I wanted President Clinton to win. I know that he wanted to raise taxes and they are being raised, but that's what's needed, actually. Clinton had a lot of good ideas about education, and me being in high school, that's one of my most important issues. Especially if I want to be a doctor—you need a good education! I wanted to vote, I really did.

*D*o you think teens care about the country? A lot of people my age care. We don't care about the same things that adults do. But they think all we care about is sex: that girl is hot or that guy is hot. That's some of the things we do care about, but there are other things we care about! We care about our nation. We don't want somebody to be president who is going to mess up the whole country.

I thought when Vice President Quayle criticized Murphy Brown, that was so stupid! There are women out there every day getting pregnant that are single parents. There are girls in high school that are doing that. Can Dan Quayle say he cares about that? No. He cares about a stupid show! Teenagers my age or whatever, fifteen, sixteen, seventeen, we care about things. We don't want the country to come to ruins.

When the Persian Gulf War first started, a lot of us teenagers were like, "Just go over and kill this person [Saddam Hussein]." I know that would be like assassination, but still. He wouldn't be threatening us today. I am worried about that because my brother's in the Navy and something could happen to him because that's where he's going. We should have just taken care of it right when it started.

*W*hich right do you value the most? Freedom of speech. When AIDS first came out, people wanted to educate others, so they wrote booklets for teenagers. They would show in detail how you could get AIDS. They would say you would get it through unprotected sex, drugs, and needles. And they would use certain words related to AIDS, like semen and drugs, and show how to actually use a real condom. That's freedom of speech and that's in your Constitution.

But they got arrested because it was vulgar language and these were high school kids. Yet it's not like kids don't speak that way anyway. Kids in our school say even worse things than semen or penis! [*Laughing*] If you want to teach high school students—this is a condom, this is how you use the condom, blah, blah, blah—it shouldn't be against the law to do that. So I think I would die before they would take freedom of speech away from me because that's just one of the freedoms that we should have.

*D*o you think there are responsibilities that come with being a citizen? With males, they have to sign up to be in the draft. I'm glad that females don't have to do that, but if there would be a war that broke out over here, I would feel obligated to help out, and probably nurse wounded soldiers or whatever. I feel obligated as it is with me being an American and also having AIDS to help people and educate them about how you get it, how you protect yourself, and what should be done.

*H*ow do you feel about your country in general? Pretty cool place. It's supposed to be a place of freedom they say, but I don't know if it's a total place of freedom. It's a place where you can try to be anything you want to be. Where they're not supposed to criticize you or discriminate against you. But there are people who do discriminate, mainly because of your race. We're all people, and it doesn't matter if you have AIDS or you're healthy. You are a person, and you deserve that right to be a person and live wherever you want to live. I'm hoping that soon this country will be a place where people don't discriminate against other people.

*I*f you could live in any country in the world, including the United States, which would you choose? Actually, I'd like to live here. We don't have just one person that rules the country; we actually have a government. They had dictatorships over in Germany and they would only have one ruler and that's it, but we have the president. While he is the main ruler, he has the vice president and you have the Congress. We have a whole bunch of people working together to run this country. I like that.

A proposal can't become a law till the Congress and the president all agree on how they want it. It goes through a whole process and the president okays it. If half the group doesn't agree with it, they would change it till it would work. Everybody works together. Here you've got freedom of speech, freedom of press. You have the Constitution. You have all those rights to protect you and other laws to punish you if you break the laws. It's just a great country.

*W*hat do you think America will be like in fifty years? If we don't do something now, the environment is going to be in bad shape in fifty years. I hope that we can do something with recycling. I know there are a lot of people out there who can't because it's expensive to recycle. You have to separate all your garbage into the right things; that's hard to do.

In fifty years, I'd like the country to be peaceful, nothing but peace. Not be any racism, discrimination, or anything. I don't want it to be where we have to pay to get something that we shouldn't have to pay for, like health care. I hope that there won't be that many diseases, and that the world and the country will be a better place.

*W*hat is your American dream? My American dream is to live long enough to be able to help people. I want to become a doctor. I don't know if I want to be a veterinarian or a pediatrician, but I want to be a doctor so I can help heal people or animals. I want the usual. I want to be a mother and a wife and be able to live a life where I can see my kids grow up. If I do pass away, I want to see them at least grow up half the way. I think that's my American dream.

"Never give up."

Dominique M. Dawes

Dominique Dawes of Silver Spring, Maryland, has felt a kind of attention that most people never experience—the roaring cheers of thousands rooting her on to triumph for the United States. As an Olympic silver medalist and world-class gymnast, she's earned much respect and 136 medals (as of spring 1993) to boot. At sixteen, Dominique is slight in size, but not in muscle, described by one journalist as a "junior Schwarzenegger." Her sweet, gentle nature, quick smile, and giggle can disguise her energy and determination, but in the gym, she's all business with poise and steely concentration. Even with all of her success, she is modest about her achievements. She attributes perfect scores to judges' generosity and refuses to class herself with other Olympians like Carl Lewis and Jackie Joyner Kersee. She worries about crime and thinks the government should invest more in children, because "we are the next leaders of America."

*H**ow did you get started in gymnastics?* I started gymnastics when I was six years old. My parents put me in the gym because I was bouncing a lot on the furniture. It was a really fun sport at that time because you just tumble and play and you're there with your friends. Right now, it's a lot more hard work and you get disappointed and frustrated a lot—because you want to be perfect.

We usually get invited to different meets almost every year, and we host a few meets. If you do well in the classics or championships, then you will go to international meets. I don't always represent the U.S.A.; I sometimes represent Hill's Gymnastics [her gym]. For the U.S.A. meets, you have to do well to go on to other countries.

If I get a 10, it's usually at invitational meets, where they score a lot easier than they do at real U.S.A. representing meets or champion-ships. So it's 10, but really I know that it's not a 10, because I got a 10 once and I had made a mistake that was really obvious. I know that they probably saw the mistake, but I was in first by so much that they probably knew giving the 10 would make me feel really proud and happy and that it would also hype the crowd.

I felt like I was working really hard the whole time in my years of gymnastics. Then, when I was about thirteen or fourteen, people were telling me that I could go to the Olympics and I wanted to work harder so that I could. When I was fifteen years old, my whole year was based on training for the Olympics. When I qualified, it was just amazing.

The Olympics was a dream come true. Barcelona [Spain] was gor-geous, though I didn't have a lot of time to go sightseeing—we were mostly training in the gym. Once the competition was over, I got time to spend with my family there, and it was fun.

And being in the Olympic village was really nice. There were other Olympic athletes and other famous people from the U.S.A., like Jackie Joyner Kersee and Carl Lewis—it was just amazing! Seeing them walk around, they were like one of us, and it was really neat. I didn't really get to talk with them, but I did get pictures of them.

At the Olympics, I wasn't really nervous for some reason, because I knew that I already qualified and I was about to compete and there was no way I was going to stop. So going for my routines, I just tried to feel confident and be my best. I had a little trouble, but overall I am just really happy.

Our last event was vault, and everyone hit well. We were hoping to come in the top three because, I believe, China was coming up close behind us. Finally, when they announced the all-around, the women's gymnastics team won a bronze medal. We were just really happy that we got a medal. That was our main goal—to do our best.

When they announced our names, we stepped on the awards stand, and everyone was in awe. That was one of the best parts of Barcelona, and now it's just like a memory that is sticking with me forever. I was hoping that I would make a final, but after that I found out [that I didn't qualify]. I was happy that it was finally over—it was great.

> **They are so young and so tiny that spectators want to pat them on the head. When their eyes narrow and their faces scrunch up with concentration, audiences go squishy with the adorableness of it all. Sports commentators cooingly label them pixies and tots, then reach for adjectives like huggable, perky, cute. Sort of like puppies. Always they are described as 'the next' Olga or Nadia or Mary Lou, as if anyone so small couldn't possibly have standing in her own right. Let's get real. The young female gymnasts who will vie for medals in Barcelona are among the world's toughest athletes.**
>
> Jill Smolowe, TIME, July 27, 1992

I love representing the U.S. and I think it's a great honor. Being there with other teammates from the U.S. makes it a lot more fun. And it's great to try your best. When I go to other competitions in other countries, or even in the U.S.A., and the U.S.A. is rooting for us, it keeps us motivated, keeps us going, and it makes us want to strive harder and go for the gold.

I hope to stay in gymnastics till the year of '94, and then get a college scholarship for four years. I either want to study medicine or criminology, but it seems to change a lot! I am not sure what I like one day or another.

I just returned from England. I was there for a week and one half, so I am about a week behind in school. I still have to train and do yesterday's schoolwork, and I still have to make up the week that I was gone. It seems like it's pretty hard that way. I like to have weekends off so I can catch up on that work, [but] I haven't had a lot of weekends off [lately] since I went to England and Utah.

I do pretty well in school, but I don't have enough time to do all the work because I miss one class to go to the gym in the morning [from 6 to 8 a.m.]. Right after school, I go back to the gym from 3 to 7 or sometimes 8, and also on Saturdays, I work out from 1 to 6. I'm taking Modern World History, Spanish, Anatomy and Physiology, Honors English, Chemistry, and Algebra II. This time I got a 3.4 average. Next year, I'll take a full six classes so I'll have enough credits to graduate.

Right now, I am just looking at the colleges' gymnastics to see which ones are the better teams. But now that I know that academics is what my future is going to consist of, I want to go to a college where they emphasize more academics and less on gymnastics. I want to spend more time discovering the fields of medicine, criminology, or law and not just keep doing gymnastics—because I don't think I'm going to be doing gymnastics when I am forty years old.

*D*o you wear red, white, and blue when you compete internationally for the United States? Usually we do, but at world championships, we are now sponsored by Reebok and the colors have changed from red, white, and blue to red, black, blue, and a pinkish. It's a really nice change, but the red, white, and blue are the American colors, so I like that a lot better.

[Reebok] supplied us with warm-ups, tennis shoes, T-shirts, leotards, and anything we need when we go on gymnastics trips. If you qualify for the national team, then you are sponsored by them. And the national team, I believe, is the top twenty girls in gymnastics.

I don't take money for endorsements. I am allowed to, but I want to get a college scholarship, and I wouldn't be able to if I took money. Some gymnasts take a lot of money, because they have won so many competitions worldwide or in the Olympics that it would really be worthwhile for them to keep it.

*Y*ou have met a lot of people from different countries. Do you have any observations on that experience—how they were different or similar? Mostly the people from different countries train exactly like we do and they just keep working on their routines. The hardest part is communicating with them. Many of them only know a little bit of English like, "Hello, how are you?" and stuff like that, like I know in Spanish. But I don't like going to countries where they know our language and we don't know anything from their language. I feel really upset when I don't know, like Russian or Chinese.

Everyone at the meets gets along really well. Before the meet, everyone wishes each other good luck or they hug each other. Then, when you get beat, they tell you to try again, or if you did really well, they congratulate you.

*W*hat is important to you? I think my fans are important to me. Most of them are gymnasts, but there are many adults who write to me too. Right after the Olympics, I got tons of mail. Most of the gymnasts ask me how to do certain skills and they congratulate me on my meets. That helps me to keep going. They write to me a lot, and many times I don't get a chance to write back. It's not that I don't care or anything, it's just that I don't have time and I have a lot of homework. I really appreciate them writing.

***W**hat was the media attention at the Olympics like?* Usually when there are a lot of people from the press hounding you, it makes you really nervous and scared. It feels like they are pressuring you, like before the competition—but really they're not. Once the competition is over, they make you feel relieved and happy. They give you great quotes and everything, and make you feel really proud of yourself.

Right after the Olympics, people were just calling a lot and writing to us, asking if they could do interviews or TV clips or stuff like that. It was really hard, but mostly before the Olympics—that was the hardest part because I was injured and I was still trying to train, and I still had to do the media stuff.

I [did get] to do a ten-second clip for Channel 4 News. That was fun. I did a round-up full dismount off the beam in like a cloudy smoke atmosphere. It was really neat and different. I didn't say anything, they just showed me doing a dismount, and then the sportscaster came up to me and started their program.

I was once on a talk show on NBC in New York with Faith Daniels. It was weird to have someone put on make-up for me, because I usually don't put a lot on. It was fun and she was really nice. We talked about the Olympics. And Kim Kelley—the gymnast that was knocked off the Olympic team—and her mom were there, and they were talking with Bela Karolyi about why she wasn't on the Olympic team. It was mostly a debate between them, but it was a great experience for me to be there.

***W**hat is it like reading about yourself in the newspaper?* I don't! I just look at the photo and critique myself 'cause I feel out of form or something [*laughing*]. I really don't read the articles, because they are all almost alike. They say, "Oh, that was just a great job, and she's dynamic," and "She started gymnastics at this and this time, and she had this much fun."

My community, like Takoma Park and Silver Spring, and Washington, D.C., really helped me out. And I do appreciate it. They have done great articles, commercial clips, and interviews. And they have been really nice and have sent me congratulations.

*H*ow has being an Olympic athlete changed your life?
You know at the Olympics I had a lot of publicity and it was great. It seemed like the whole world just changed in a heartbeat. [When] I went to the mall a few times and people recognized me, I [would have]

Even though gymnastics has always been included in modern Olympic Games, women weren't permitted to compete individually until 1952. Women's events include the uneven parallel bars, the balance beam, floor exercise, and the vault.

like an autograph session. But now, I'm glad that it's calmed down and back to normal, and that I can just be a normal person that can go out somewhere and not be mobbed.

*W*hat would you tell gymnastics fans about living a life as a gymnastics competitor? I tell them that it is a lot of hard work. Even though you don't get a lot of sleep—I'm used to five or six hours of sleep and I couldn't get ten or twelve hours, that would be way too much—you always have to keep trying hard. Even when you get frustrated, and it's really hard to come back—you do. Pain is the number one struggle that we have. I have had a strained hamstring, a shoulder injury, and two ankles with tendinitis.

During the Olympics, I had tendinitis in my ankle the whole time. But when it was the Olympics, I didn't think anything was going to stop me from competing. So I just kept trying to train. Afterwards I was able to get my ankle casted, and now the tendinitis is gone.

*I*f you had the choice of living anywhere in the world—including the United States—where would you choose to live? I've visited Holland, England,

France, and Spain. For places around the U.S.A., I've been almost everywhere, except for Seattle, Oregon, Idaho, and Michigan. I would probably like to live in Holland, because that was one of the funnest trips that I had. We didn't get to go very far into the city, but we got to see a little bit of what was there. And their cultures and everything were pretty much like ours or New Orleans. I would rather live in America like I am now, but if I had to pick somewhere else it would be Holland.

*W*hat is your definition of an American? Probably a person who believes in their rights for America. They listen to the government. They also vote and they want to help control the government.

*W*hat do you consider your most cherished right as an American? [*Pause*] Probably the right to vote. You have a say in who is going to control you in the U.S.A. Once you learn about them, you can vote for [the candidate that you like best].

*D*o you think you have responsibilities as an American? I think that everyone should just follow the laws, pay their taxes, make their money, have their job, and just live an everyday life. Vote and control their government.

No one should own guns at all. I think it's ridiculous what people do. It's usually the person that owns [a gun] who gets it used on them. I think if everyone owns a gun or is able to own a gun, then everyone will end up shooting each other over ridiculous situations. But if no one owns a gun, there is no one to shoot at because you won't have that firearm. And it's better that way. I think that maybe just the police should have them, for more violent cases.

*D*o you think that the government is doing a good job? I don't keep up with the government a lot, but I think that they are. But all I've been hearing about is violence in the world, like things in Waco [Texas] and stuff like that. And it's disappointing to hear things like that 'cause I think that the government or the people should be able to control it.

If you could change one thing about the government, what would it be? I know that the government probably puts a lot into America, but I would like to see them putting stronger emphasis on crime and things that happen in households, cities, or gangs—and not just go into foreign affairs right away when another country is starving. We have a lot of people in America that are born addicted to things and with diseases. I think we should help ourselves and think of better cures for diseases and put more emphasis on scientists.

I think the police are doing a great job, but I think the people in the world can all police themselves. If you train everyone to look out for others and to love one another, then we wouldn't need police.

What do you think of the situation in some inner cities, where there is a lot of poverty and drugs? I think it's really sad to hear about that on the news, how they are shooting each other, or how people are just found dead on the street because of drugs. I wish there was a way that we could control the drug intake and not let a lot of it come in at once. We can't just deprive them totally of drugs—they would go crazy. But we could just allow them a little at a time and maybe it will be all gone.

In the Rodney King trial, it was obvious that the LAPD was guilty. I think that the policemen should serve their time so that it would show other police officers that they can't just beat up on someone— just 'cause they raise an arm or something. I mean, on the videotape it shows that he's just trying to protect himself, and they keep beating on him. I think they are guilty.

What do you think about discrimination issues in this country? I think pretty much everything is equal right now, but it's just some people are brought up racist. I think that's sad. But they must have been taught that in their families because the government today seems as if everything is pretty equal. I do see it improving a lot.

*M*any people were excited about your going to the Olympics because you were the first African-American gymnast to be on the team. What did you think about that? Well, I felt that all of my training paid off. I was just really happy that I qualified, and I never thought about the part that I was the first black gymnast until someone told me. It was a great honor.

*D*id you have a favorite candidate in the presidential election last fall? Well, at first I wanted Bush to win. But after people were so disappointed that he promised us no new taxes—which is a mistake for him to say—then when he raised taxes, I think that dropped him a lot. I don't think there was any way they could not raise taxes. Then I was really rooting for Perot, but my parents voted for Clinton. I am really happy that Clinton won. I didn't really know much about any of them, except for Bush—I wasn't really paying attention 'cause of the Olympics.

*Y*ou got to meet President Bush, right? Yes, after the Olympics, all the U.S. Olympians were invited to the White House to meet President Bush and Barbara Bush. It was really fun. It was pretty crowded, and it was supposed to be a picnic, but it started storming, so we went inside and we had hot dogs and hamburgers.

We never really got to meet him [Bush]. We just saw him, and he gave a speech and congratulated all of us. It was just great that he would spend time to talk to us, instead of just [spending time] on foreign affairs.

*D*o you trust politicians? I don't really listen to politicians. I don't think I get into politics a lot. I think whatever decisions that our House of Representatives makes is to better us, and they wouldn't make decisions that would hurt us. They are just trying to help us because they live in this community also.

*H*ow does the government affect your life? Well, many times it makes my life a lot easier, like if they control crimes and stuff like that. But many times, they make my life a lot harder like if they have to raise taxes. My dad or mom takes me to the gym everyday, and when gas prices go up, it's a lot harder for us to pay for it, and it's hard for me to make it to the gym.

*W*ho are your heroes? I think my heroes are the Lord, and also my mom and father—because I've learned a lot of things from them, and they keep me going. They really help me in the world. They tell me right from wrong, and they try to discipline me a lot and will not let it slide, or say, "Oh, don't worry about it, you won't do it again." They'll punish me!

*H*ow would you describe yourself? I'm usually happy, but I am *very* stubborn. I am determined in what I do. Usually if someone wants me to do something and I don't want to do it, I won't do it. But usually it will come along that I have to do it. [*Laughing*] Like chores!

*W*hat's your American dream? My American dream is just having a successful career and being able to live on my own. I want to be very independent and not be dependent on other people, so that if they leave me, that I won't just be left with nothing. I guess that is my dream.

*W*hat kind of advice would you give your grandkids about life? I would tell them to learn from other people's mistakes and to always look around you, not just straight ahead—look around at what's going on in the world today. Always set goals, try to reach for your future, and never give up.

*W*hat do you think the country will be like in fifty years? Hopefully there will be no racism in the world, and no one will have a gun in their house at all. And violence and crime in America will be depleted. There will be no more starvation in the world. This is kind of thinking of a perfect world that I would want live in—but I think we can do it in fifty years.

*W*hy did you agree to do this interview? Well, I think this is an interesting thing to let people know how teens feel about the U.S. government right now. Many times people don't ask teenagers how they feel because they don't think teens have enough knowledge to care at all—they just think teens only care about school and their friends and other clubs.

I think that a lot of Americans do care about their country, but they don't admit it because they are so hooked up in their jobs or families that they just don't pay attention. But yes, they really do care for the country.

"You gotta be looking to get a step ahead."

Dan Helfrich

It wasn't easy playing President George Bush in the school mock election, but somebody had to do it. And if anyone could rise to the challenge, it would surely be sixteen-year-old Dan Helfrich. What did he learn? "I realized that politics was a lot more intricate than I thought." Having moved more than seven times before settling into his current home in Avon, Connecticut, with his parents and three brothers, Dan has learned to make friends easily, adjust to new situations, and appreciate the solid foundation his family has given him. Dan is also grateful for the top-notch education he is receiving at the Loomis Chaffee Academy prep school. He's opinionated, athletic, and loves sports broadcasting, so look for Dan in about four years—he may be coming to a station near you. While his own future success seems assured, Dan wants the American dream to come true for all Americans, and he hopes to see the day when bias will finally disappear and an African American or a woman becomes president.

Tell me about your relationship with your family. There is definitely a lot of love in my family and a lot of mutual respect between the parents and the kids and between the four brothers. I hear horror stories from my friends about parents that are really strict. My parents definitely have some authority, but they're approachable and I feel like I can talk to them about anything. In some ways, I think they're an emotional crutch for me, maybe, and they're always going to be there. Going to school now at Loomis, I'm away a lot. I leave home at seven in the morning and I don't get back until seven at night, but when I get home, I know there are people I can talk to.

The commute [to Loomis] is thirty-five minutes each way, which gets to be a little long sometimes. You might say, why am I doing this? But I don't think there's any way I could leave my family because I've spent my whole life at home and it's such a comfortable environment for me. I get homesick when I go away to camp for a week in the summer just because I like to sleep in my own bed and talk to my dad at night. To be a boarder at school would have eliminated a big part of my life, really. Being a day student allows me to have the best of both worlds.

> **I had a negative view of prep schools as snobby, exclusive, and elitist. But after a neighbor's repeated urging, we toured Loomis. And it began to change my mind. The campus was collegiate, the student body diverse, and the people very open and friendly.**
>
> Mary Sue Helfrich, Dan's mom

There's an aura about Loomis. The people are very welcoming and very friendly, and you get a feeling that there's something special about the place. That's pretty much what made up my decision to go there. Another one of the main factors was that my parents and I wanted an academic challenge for me.

The first couple of weeks of fall term, you're incredibly nervous. I was used to spending my whole day inside one building, as everybody else is, at a public school. At Loomis, you're on such a big campus, and you don't have classes periods one through seven; you have probably three or four classes a day, which means you have three free periods. There is also diversity at the school in that we have a large enough endowment that kids can come in on financial aid. You get kids from the city and kids that don't have the money to afford it. I think a lot of people find that making friends is pretty easy at Loomis because it's a situation where most people don't know a lot of other people. Most of the friends that I had in my freshman year are still my good friends now.

Academically, it's a huge difference. I went through middle school getting straight As, not being challenged at all, and not doing more than twenty-five minutes of homework a night. The teachers here are very knowledgeable about their subject areas and teach them very well. They demand a lot more of you than I had ever been asked for before. My grades my freshman year were probably B-pluses, Bs, A-minuses. That's very good for the school. The curriculum at Loomis also allows you to make a lot of different choices, and there's an incredible amount of flexibility. I think that I'll come out of Loomis with a lot broader knowledge and a lot more resources than someone would come out of Avon High School with.

Do you feel that you're privileged? Well, I live in a very nice suburban neighborhood and a very nice house, and on TV, I see homeless people or people in the inner city—when you see something like that, you know that you're privileged.

The other way I'd say I'm privileged is because of my family. There's a lot of my friends who don't have the foundation that I have because of my family, and I think that's been a big part of my life. I also think I'm privileged because of my friends. I never had friendships growing up to the strength of the ones I have now, and I hope they will last for a lifetime. So I think I'm privileged in a lot of ways, not just financially—there's a lot of love in my life.

Are there things that you try to do to take advantage of or to appreciate what you have? Well, I like to be actively involved; I don't like to sit around and watch TV a lot. So when I'm not in school, I try to do different things. I'm a lector at St. Anne's Parish. I wrote the pastor a letter and said, "I'd like to do this; I don't feel as involved as I think I should be in my church," and now I'm the only youth lector they've ever had.

I also coach my little brother's soccer team outside of school, about twelve eight-year-old kids, which is a lot of fun. Soccer's been a big part of my life, and I feel like the experience of playing any sport when you're young is invaluable. I like to help the kids out, and I enjoy being with them, so that's a natural connection for me.

There's a great sense of accomplishment when someone—maybe a less-talented athlete—scores a goal or makes a good play, and he comes over and gives me a high-five. That means a lot to me. Like last year, we had a kid on our team named James who suffered from mild cerebral palsy. We had a penalty kick late in the game, and my brother Brian's a good goal scorer and a great player, and he was about to take it. I said, "No, let James take it." So he takes the penalty kick, and he puts it in. And as he was running over to the stands to hug his parents, I thought, "God, this was a special moment for me," because I felt like I had a part in it. To see someone like that succeed means a lot to me.

*W*ould you be eligible to try out for the Olympic soccer team? It's a long, drawn-out process. The Olympic team is comprised of people who have come up through the Olympic development system. I am an Olympic development player for the state of Connecticut. If you make the state team, you can go to a regional team. People that are on regional teams can then be taken into a national pool. Once you are in a national pool, then you'll be given a chance to prove yourself.

I made the state team and the regional team. I am eligible for the national team, but I didn't make it this year. Now, with my regional team, I am going to go to England in April. For me, the Olympics has always been something I would have loved to have done, but they passed a new rule this year for soccer where you have to be under twenty-three to play in the Olympics, and I would be twenty-three the year I would play. The next Olympics in '96, I would be nineteen, and I would never make it 'cause I'd be too young. It's kind of a bummer.

A*re you interested in playing professionally?* Nah—I want to get out of college and get into the workforce and do something. My dad's in human resources, and that field interests me because I like working with people and the whole business scene kind of intrigues me.

Another thing I'd love to do is to be a journalist because I love writing and English; they're my best subjects in school. But the career I've always wanted is to be a sports broadcaster. I've been on the radio twice, hosting a sports talk show in Connecticut.

W*here did you learn about government?* In U.S. history class I've learned a lot about government. Mr. Andrian, my teacher, is a great teacher. He knows the government system really well, and he can teach that really well. But I think I get a lot of my knowledge of and my interest in government from media like TV and newspapers. CNN and C-SPAN are on a lot at my house. Government has always interested me.

The most hands-on experience with government I've had was this fall when we had a mock presidential election for the whole school. Mr. Andrian basically appointed me to play George Bush, but also I wanted to. Everybody had a role, so I had my own wife, vice president, secretary of state, campaign manager, and secret service guys. There was a debate every Friday in the quadrangle at my school in front of 100 or 200 kids. There is random questioning from the audience, so you had to learn to speak on your feet. I used to think that Clinton and Bush were dancing around the issues in a debate; but I found myself doing the same thing, which was sort of embarrassing. Somebody asked me a specific thing about welfare that I hadn't read anything about, and I just said, "Well, we're doing a lot for cities and we're working hard to establish enterprise zones and unemployment rates are falling," and then the guy said, "Well, you're not answering my question!" I said, "I know!" So I gained a little more respect for candidates and realized that politics is a little more intricate than I may have thought. That's the best experience I've had at Loomis.

*W*ell, based on your experience in the mock election, how do you think George Bush did in the real thing? Bush tried his best. He was against the wall from the beginning. After the Gulf War, his approval ratings were sky high and then as things were turned to the domestic front, slowly the approval ratings went down and unfortunately for him, it came to a point where the recession was the foremost thing on the average voter's mind. That climaxed right at the time the campaign started, so he's in a position where he's in a lot of trouble and it's hard to find a defense for that when the statistics don't lie; there'd been a real fall-off in a lot of economic figures since he took office. I would contend that if the Gulf War would have happened in December of 1991, George Bush wins the election. The amount of national pride, togetherness, and nationalism shown after the Gulf War would have served him perfect in the campaign, but it didn't work out. I think Clinton's whole message of change struck some chords in the American citizens' eyes.

Perot hurt Bush a lot too, because Perot attracted a lot of attention and he focused a lot more on attacking Bush with wild accusations or whatever and attacking Bush's record than he did attacking Clinton's record as governor.

You have to appeal to the people. Campaigning isn't a strict, cut-and-dry, issue-related forum, and I don't think Bush displayed enthusiasm—he was kind of lackluster and blah. It seemed like he had kind of given up, maybe, and then he had this resurgence at the end where he starts attacking Clinton, but it was too late.

*Y*our teacher, Mr. Andrian, thought you handled the campaign better than the real George Bush. [*Laughter*] That was one of the best compliments I have ever gotten. The headmaster said, "Bush would have won if he had your enthusiasm." That meant a lot to me.

*W*hat kind of role do you think the media played in the election? The media plays a huge role in any election, and I think the media gave Bush an incredibly hard time in this one. If you take the stereotypical journalist or the stereotypical broadcaster, he is liberal in nature and Democratic; so I think the media has a natural prejudice to kind of subliminally supporting the Democrats. Also, at a press conference, you're not going to find lower-class or middle-class people. Those people who are White House correspondents or journalists for CNN and NBC—they're asking specific questions, mainly about economic plans and foreign affairs, because they are all making six figures a year. So I don't think the media itself has a whole lot of diversity within its population.

The other thing was that Ross Perot was kind of a media candidate and they spent a lot of time writing about Perot and promoting him as a candidate who had a lot to say. As far as I'm concerned, the more you can hear people talk about your issues, then the better educated you are to make a decision when it comes to voting time.

*H*ow did going through the mock election affect your views on politics? I think politics should be more issue-geared and presidential elections and campaigns are poorly run—there's a lot of propaganda. I think politicians are way too much influenced by what their party believes. When they're making a decision, they have to compromise their beliefs for fear of alienating someone in their own party or some special interest group somewhere. I think that's wrong, and George Bush proves it perfectly—before he was the vice presidential candidate for Reagan, he was a firm believer in pro-choice and then, just to salvage his political career, he changed instantaneously to pro-life to go along with the position of the Republican party. A lot of the decisions politicians make are geared towards what's going to happen in four years, and that's why things aren't getting done.

*W*as there a lot of interest in the campaign on your campus? An incredible amount. I'll tell you the one issue that garners by far the most attention is abortion. I think it is unrepresentative of the nation as a whole. I think the audience at Loomis was so geared toward abortion and so pro-choice as a whole—as most high schools are, and especially prep schools, which are pretty liberal—that it was hard to be George Bush. Some people got angry with me. Even when I was out of character attending classes, they would challenge me to discussions about abortion. I said, "Listen, I'm just playing a guy!"

There were times when it was hard, but I kind of liked being the underdog. I got the crowd into it—I was loud and said some pretty harsh things about the other two guys just to get their attention so they wouldn't dismiss me from the outset. That was kind of fun.

People didn't have to show up to our debates that we had, but they were really into it, and there's a lot of kids of voting age that came up to me and said that the mock election at school really helped them in making a decision about who to vote for. Some high school kids don't pay that much attention to things, but when they are given an opportunity to hear about it and it's something they can relate to, then they can make a better decision.

If I were a voter in the real election, I would have first of all been disgusted with the three choices, but I would have voted for Bush. Clinton kinda scared me. He tries to give government a little more control than is necessary. He thinks the government should regulate everything. Clinton spent half his time in the election talking about "read my lips," and I would have done so too, but Clinton has broken his tax pledge, too! It kind of disturbs me—the length that people will go to to win elections.

So how would you describe the leadership you would like to see in the president? I think you gotta have a person of courage, first and foremost: someone that's not afraid of what other people are gonna say and that's gonna get things done. There's so much focus on party alignment, [which causes] so much gridlock in government. People are so concerned with "What am I going to vote for on this issue because the Democrats are gonna have this position and the Republicans this position?" Until that disappears, then we're in trouble.

The president should be someone who is a good leader in that he is respected by the people in Congress, by lobbyists, and most importantly, by the American people. He's gotta be someone who is going to stick by his convictions, and I think Bill Clinton may be classified a little bit as a wimp because he easily backs down—I think someone like that probably isn't in the best position to lead our country.

I consider myself independent. I'm probably more inclined to the Republican party, but for me to associate myself firmly with a party would seem that I believe in everything they support, and I don't. If everybody was independent, if there was no registering of voters, then I think you would have a lot more honesty and a lot more people at election time considering the issues, considering the people running for election and their integrity, and not looking at the "R" or the "D" next to the person's name.

The two-party system doesn't allow for the expression of many beliefs in our country. African Americans are poorly represented in either party. Native Americans are completely ignored; homosexuals—the Republican party disowns them. Party politics doesn't allow the people of the United States, and the diversity and the melting pot of the United States, to be represented.

How do you think we are doing on discrimination issues in this country? Well, the LA riots give heat to the fact that there are some unhappy people in the country. I think rather than take a firm stance or trying to do something, the Democratic and Republican parties fear trying to reach out to the people in the cities, because what are the affluent people in their party going to think? Those people are the ones paying the money and comprise more of the party. So they say, "We're doing all we can"—but what are they really doing? I think in our country there's been a long history of discrimination against certain people. The affluent white male has always been the dominant figure in society, and the woman has always been ignored through history. That's starting to change, which is good.

Do you think there are things that ordinary people can do to make changes in discriminatory behavior? No, I think the main problem is that they can't. All legislation starts from the hierarchy and the political aristocracy in Washington, D.C., and I don't think [minorities] are represented there. I think the only way that African Americans have been heard is through the LA riots—and I shouldn't even say the African Americans, but the people in the city, the urban people. I think that's a terrible thing that they can't be represented in the government. The lobbyists aren't speaking for those people, either.

*D*o you think politicians are trustworthy? Anyone who has the knowledge and the background of most of the politicians is trustworthy enough. However, I think it all goes back to the fact that once you're locked into the system of big-time politics, you get cajoled into supporting things in your [party] platform. In that case, politicians are not trustworthy because what they are saying isn't necessarily what they're believing. That is exactly what Bush did.

*D*o you think you would want to be in a political office yourself? No, because I fear exactly what I just talked about. I'm someone who is strong in my convictions and there are so many factors influencing people in politics—there's lobbyists, special interest groups, the president, and the Senate majority leader, or whatever. It scares me that I wouldn't be able to win an election unless I compromised my beliefs. That's not something I'd be willing to do.

*W*hat is your most cherished right as an American? I think it is probably the right to vote, which I haven't experienced yet since I'm not eighteen. The privilege of being able to have a hand in electing the people that are going to make the decisions and the laws is a right that a lot of people in a lot of countries don't have. It's something unique to the democratic nations of the world and I think people take for granted the right to vote. There's not enough people in the cities that vote at election time, and in 1988 only 50 percent of the registered voters actually voted. If everyone cherished their right to vote—like I feel they should—then I think you'd have a more representative Senate and Congress.

So how would you describe a good citizen? A good citizen isn't afraid to challenge what's going on in his country, and a good citizen is aware of what's going on in the country. A good citizen tries, in the way in which he can do best and using the talent which he has, to let people know what he feels is wrong or right. If you're just going to sit down and watch CNN and C-SPAN and say, "Well, that's not very good, that's terrible!" but you're not going to do anything, then what good are you as a voter? And how are you going to make a change unless you start to effect the change yourself? The American people are so hesitant to speak up and they think, "Well, I'm not going to be heard." You saw that in this election when there was so much talk about wasting a vote. How can you waste a vote? You can't do it! [*Frustrated*] The vote says to the people in Washington, D.C., that 25 percent of the people believed in Ross Perot. Don't we need to change things a little bit to provide for the beliefs of the people who voted for him?

What do you think the biggest problem facing the country is today? [*Long pause*] We've always prided ourselves on our country, and you always hear our country being dubbed the "melting pot," for we have a lot of different races, religions, and cultures represented in our population. But I think the biggest problem facing our country is that generally white males control the political system. And when you are that disproportionately unrepresentative of the whole citizenship of a country, you face alienating a number of people. And I think the United States, unless it gets something done—I'm not educated enough and knowledgeable enough to know what that is—faces some serious divisions amongst its own citizens, and that could take a real violent turn. I think we saw a glimpse of that in LA. I just think the racial diversity of our country should be used as an asset, and right now I fear that it's going to ultimately be a disadvantage and lead to some problems.

Everybody voting and citizens expressing what they believe—it all comes into the big picture, but half the problem is the people in the inner city don't have the education and are not getting the education that they need to hold political office or to be heard, respected, and believed. Unless they're gonna be given the opportunity to do that, then you're in trouble.

*I*f you could change something about the government, what would it be? If I had a wish one day . . . it would be that the government would take more seriously their influence on the lives of the people in their country. And ultimately, by the end of my life, I would love to see a woman president or an African-American president or a Native American president, and I don't think right now that that's a legitimate opportunity. My wishes are real idealistic ones—that everyone would be represented in government and that the events that happen in Washington, D.C., and big-time politics would be more faithful and more representative of the population in this country.

*W*ho are your heroes? Well, my heroes are my grandfather, who fought in the Marines in World War II. He's a wonderful guy today, and he's great to talk to. And my father, who is a real honest guy. I think he's done a lot for people. And my mother—she's a real giving person, and I think she has bettered the lives of a lot of people. In a more public sense, my heroes are guys like Jim Valvano, the former basketball coach who has cancer now.* He's a man of great courage; he's fighting through the cancer and speaking out about it, saying, "Cancer research isn't given enough money. AIDS is getting ten times as much research funding as cancer, and it's not fair." And Arthur Ashe is an inspirational guy; he did a lot with his life. Martin Luther King is absolutely my ultimate hero. I get, like [*pause*] emotional . . . every time I hear the "I Have A Dream" speech because for me, he did more for a certain race of people than anyone that I have come across.

*D*o you think you could make a difference? Yeah, I'd like to think I could make a difference. I've been given the opportunity to get a great education at a great school. I'll hopefully go on to a great college, and that's an opportunity in itself. If you're given an opportunity, I think it's my responsibility to do something, whether it's in the

---

Jim Valvano died in April 1993 of cancer.

media, as a lawyer, or as a sports announcer. In some way you have to take a burden upon yourself to take the privileged life that I've had and to translate it into doing something for the country. Too many people don't take that responsibility seriously enough.

Have you heard the term "American dream"? What's yours? The American dream—that everyone is gonna be free and someone can come over from Ireland when there was a potato famine and have equal opportunity—that's what I consider the proverbial American dream.

But my American dream is that everyone else's American dream would come true and that there wouldn't be so much underlying prejudice in this nation. My American dream is to see an African American in the White House. I think that would be a great thing. It would show me how far we have come. Also my American dream is that my children and my grandchildren are going to be able to experience the privileges and the love that I've experienced in my life. I've only lived sixteen years—but I'm real lucky and I wish that everyone could be as lucky as I've been and could be given the opportunities that I've been given.

What do you see for your own personal future? What do you want to do in your life? I want to get married! I want to go to college, get married, get a job, and be happy. I would be happy if I lived in a stable family where I had a great relationship with my wife and saw my parents and brothers a lot. And if I had a good home and my kids were afforded the opportunity to have a good education and I was employed.

Why were you interested in doing this interview? Well, I'm an opinionated person. [*Laughing*] My mom always says, any chance I get to talk I could never turn down. And "who cares what I think?"—it's kind of a mentality that you hear echoed a lot by kids my age because I don't think they're being represented. If I'm given a chance here to represent teenagers, then I think I'm doing my generation a service.

***W**hat do you think the country will be like in fifty years?* We're going in the right direction, but history will tell you that things take a long time to work themselves out. The abolition of slavery is a huge accomplishment for history, and it's a huge accomplishment that African Americans and women have the right to vote today—that took a real long time. And those are changes that we take for granted, too. A lot of progress has been made since the Revolutionary War, or even since the days when Columbus came. So, in fifty years? I don't see a lot different than today. But things are going to change in history; there hasn't been a point in history where things have not changed.

I'd like to be considered an optimist, so I have a good feeling about the future. The people of my generation are more outspoken and more in tune with what's going on, and I'd like to think that when the people of my generation are in the position that the people that in politics are in today, they're gonna be more sensitive and more representative of the people of our country. I think a lot of progress has been made in that regard. But more and more needs to be done; you can never say that's good enough. You gotta be looking to get a step ahead.

***I**f you had the opportunity to live in any country in the world, including the United States, which would you choose?* I love the United States, because as many negative things or as many picky things as I've said about the way our country works, in reality it's one of the most forward-thinking, democratic countries in the world. I think the United States is probably the best place for my kids to grow up. I don't think there is another country like the United States in the world.